·TESCO· COOKERY· COLLECTION·
WINES AND COCKTAILS

Written by Norma Macmillan

Illustrations by Jane Strother

Map artwork by Eugene Fleury

Additional assistance from Adrian Lane
and the Wines and Spirits department at Tesco

Published exclusively for Tesco Stores Ltd,
Delamare Road, Cheshunt, Herts EN8 9SL
by Cathay Books, 59 Grosvenor Street, London W1

First published 1986

© Cathay Books 1986

ISBN 0 86178 396 4

Printed in Hong Kong

ACKNOWLEDGEMENTS

The publishers would like to thank the following who
were concerned in the preparation of the book

Series Art Director Pedro Pra-Lopez
Photographer Chris Crofton (page 28 Patrick Eagar)
Stylist Maria Kelly
Drinks prepared for photography by Nichola Palmer
Special editorial help Andrew Jefford

CONTENTS

NOTE

The measure used in all the recipes is based on
a standard 'jigger' which is approximately 45 ml (1½ fl oz).
If preferred the volume can be adjusted
providing the proportions are kept the same.

Standard spoon measurements are used in all recipes
1 tablespoon (tbls) = one 15 ml spoon
1 teaspoon (tsp) = one 5 ml spoon
All spoon measures are level

For all recipes, quantities are given in both metric and imperial measure.
Follow either set but not a mixture of both, as they are not interchangeable.

Most of the cocktail recipes call for ice either crushed or cubed.
If you wish to use ice check there is plenty available in your freezer.

Following the success of the first 12 books we produced in the Tesco Cookery Collection, we are delighted to be adding 8 new titles to this exciting series. As before, it is the close contact we have with our customers and the feedback we have had through our Consumer Advisory Kitchens which has helped us to select these latest titles. Each one focuses on an area in which our customers have shown particular interest and contains practical information, colourful illustrations and a wide selection of recipes.

Wines and Cocktails aims to take the mystique out of wine drinking. These days, wines and spirits are readily available in shops and stores, but many people find the vast range rather daunting. This book describes and illustrates the grape varieties and the different regions of the main wine-producing countries – and the vintage chart will advise you on the best years to buy. There is a section on the range of wine packaging available to help you choose the most convenient type. The fully illustrated Cocktails section is all about fun and frivolity, mixing drinks for colour as well as for taste.
I hope you will enjoy looking through *Wines and Cocktails* and developing your knowledge of this fascinating subject. Cheers!

Carey Dennis, chief home economist, Tesco Stores Ltd.

Introduction

All over the world, millions of people drink a glass of wine as casually as we British have a cup of tea or a pint of beer. We are beginning to enjoy wine more and more, but too many of us still believe that an easy familiarity with it only comes with specialist knowledge.

Wine was brought to Britain by the Romans and was made here throughout the Middle Ages. After the acquisition of Bordeaux and the vineyards there, in 1153, the flourishing winemaking trade in Britain came to an end, but the British continued to drink vast quantities of imported wines. Despite this, wine is still too often surrounded by mystique and snobbishness.

What is wine?
Wine is the fermented juice of crushed, freshly picked grapes. During the fermentation, the natural sugar in the grape juice is converted into alcohol by the yeast found on the grape skins, and the juice is transformed into wine.

Growing
The grapes that are used to make wine need careful nurturing, but the conditions for growing top quality wine grapes are, in agricultural terms, somewhat unusual. Most of the world's best wine-making regions do not have lush, fertile soil or unlimited sunshine. Instead, vines will only produce fine grapes if they have had to struggle to survive. To ripen, grapes need warm, sunny summers, with just enough rain to keep the grapes juicy, and cool winters. Any extremes of temperature can cause great damage.

Making wine
To make red wine, black or purple grapes are used, and the crushed grape skins are left with the pressed juice during the fermentation process, to give colour. The skins also provide tannin – an important preservative as well as a taste-enhancer.

White wines are usually made from white or green grape varieties (although in Champagne, white wine is made from black grapes). After pressing out the juice, the grape skins are soon discarded, unless the winemaker wants his wine to keep well. In this case, the skins are left in for a short period to increase the tannin content and, in some cases, aromatic oils are added for flavour.

Rosé wines can be made by two methods: by fermenting black grapes with their skins just long enough to impart the right colour, or by fermenting a mixture of black and white grapes, with the skins. Because the tannin content will be low, rosé wines should be drunk when young.

Most red table wines are fermented until virtually all the sugar is gone – thus they taste dry. Some sweet white wines, on the other hand, have their fermentation stopped before all the sugar has been used up.

After the fermentation, the wine is put into small barrels or large tanks to age – for a few weeks or up to 3 years or more, depending on local custom. Finally it is filtered and bottled. It will continue to age in the bottle.

What is a vintage?
A vintage is the year in which wine grapes are harvested and made into wine, so 'vintage wines' are those that bear a date on their labels. Some vintage wines are for drinking as soon as possible – for example light, white wines like Muscadet or Frascati. Others – like fine red Bordeaux or Bourgogne (burgundy) – will go on improving in the bottle for several years, particularly when the vintage is a good one (see page 25).

Grape Varieties

The species *Vitis vinifera*, from a huge family of climbing plants, is the vine almost invariably grown for wine grapes. Within this species there are a number of different grape varieties, and each wine producer selects those for growing which will be best suited to the climate and soil in his vineyards.

Some wine is made from a single grape variety, but many are produced by blending together the juices of several complementary varieties. This blending requires great skill if it is to make the best use of the qualities of the different grapes. Many of the world's great wines are produced from blends of two or more grape varieties.

Because different grape varieties contribute so much to the taste of wine, and because many bottles of wine are labelled according to the grape variety from which they are made, a basic knowledge of them is useful. Here are some of the principal grape varieties grown around the world:

Left: Pinot Noir, and right: Gamay. Both show light to medium depth of colour, suggesting lively, fruity tastes

RED WINE VARIETIES

Cabernet Sauvignon: grown all over the world, from Bordeaux to California and Australia; produces fine wines that keep well; often blended; the resulting wine has deep colour and fruity flavour reminiscent of blackcurrants.

Gamay: grown in the Beaujolais region and in California, where it is sometimes blended; produces light wines that do not keep well; the resulting wine is fruity with a light purple-pink colour.

Grenache: grown in France in the Southern Rhône, Languedoc and Côtes de Provence, as well as in California, Australia and Rioja in Spain where it is called *garnacha*; produces light, fruity, red and rosé wines that will keep moderately well.

Merlot: grown in Bordeaux and in California; blended with Cabernet Sauvignon to make fine clarets; also grown in Italy to produce soft, fruity wine.

Nebbiolo: The splendid Nebbiolo grape is grown to the North West of Italy and produces wines that are softer, and more

Left: Syrah, and right: Cabernet Sauvignon. Greater depth of colour indicates the tannin and extract of full-bodied wine

mellow than the better known Barola.

Pinot Noir: grown in Burgundy as well as the West Coast of the United States; it produces fine, medium-bodied wine that keeps well; also used to make Champagne.

Syrah: grown in the Northern Rhône region, in California and in Australia where it is called Shiraz; produces strong, heavy wine with a deep colour; some is very fine and will keep well.

WHITE WINE VARIETIES

Chardonnay: grown in Burgundy and California; produces fine wines that keep well; resulting wine can vary in colour from pale greenish yellow to deep yellow, and is usually full-bodied and dry; used to make Champagne.

Chenin Blanc: grown in the middle Loire region as well as in California: produces wine that can be kept, if well made; the resulting wine is delicate, and medium-dry to sweet.

Gewürztraminer: grown in the Alsace region, Germany, Austria, Northern Italy and California; produces aromatic, spicy

wine that does not usually keep well; the resulting wine can be fairly dry to slightly sweet.

Müller-Thurgau: grown in Germany, Austria and England; new variety that produces flowery, soft white wines.

Muscat: One of the world's most important grape varieties, grown in nearly every wine-producing country. There are two distinct styles of wine produced: in Alsace the wine is dry, whereas in the South of France and elsewhere the wine is sweet and high in alcohol.

Riesling: grown all over the world, from the Alsace region and Germany to Australia and California; produces fine wines, the best of which can be kept; the resulting wine is usually dry to medium-dry, but also used to make fine sweet dessert wines.

Sauvignon Blanc: grown in the Loire and Bordeaux regions of France as well as in California where it is sometimes called Fumé Blanc; produces dry, aromatic wines (Sancerre, Pouilly Fumé); or may be used in sweet (Barsac, Sauternes); Loire wines should be drunk young: Bordeaux wines keep well.

Left: Chenin Blanc, right: Gewürztraminer. Light and medium colour indicates delicacy of taste; the wines may be dry or sweet

Left: Chardonnay, and right: dessert Muscat. Medium colour indicates a full-bodied white and deeper colour indicates sweet wine

Bottle Shapes

There are several classic bottle shapes that can sometimes tell you what wine they contain. The wine-producing regions of France and Germany still use the bottle shapes first associated with them. However, wine producers all over the world have now adapted these classic bottle shapes for their own use, so this is not a foolproof guide to use in identifying wines except those from France and Germany.

The classic **Bordeaux** bottle is tall, with strong, high shoulders. It is made of dark green glass, except in the case of sweet white wines, when the glass used is clear. The classic medium or sweet **sherry** bottle is similar, with a longer neck.

The classic **Burgundy** bottle (also sometimes used in the Loire region) is tall and slope-shouldered. It is made of light brown glass for red wines and of green or clear glass for white wines.

The classic **Champagne** bottle is similar in shape to the Burgundy bottle, but it is larger due to the thickness of the glass used.

The classic **Côtes-du-Rhône** bottle is shorter and squatter than the Bordeaux and Burgundy bottles, and is slope-shouldered.

There are two bottle shapes used in **Provence**. One is very tall with an undulating shape, somewhat like a figure eight with a long neck. The other slopes gently from a narrow top to a wider bottom, somewhat like a pear.

The classic bottle shape used in the **Alsace** region of France is also used in **Germany**. It is a slim, shoulderless, tall bottle. For Alsace and Moselle wines, the glass is green; for Rhine wines the glass is brown.

Traditionally, **Chianti** was put into rounded squat bottles set in straw baskets; these are being replaced by brown glass Bordeaux-type bottles.

Other Wines

SPARKLING WINES

Champagne and other sparkling wines are usually reserved for special occasions and celebrations though there is no good reason why they should not be drunk at any time! The Benedictine monk, Dom Perignon, is credited with having invented Champagne in the seventeenth century. He devised a cork to replace the pegs and rags that were originally used to stopper the bottles of wine, and discovered that this effectively retained the natural sparkle. In fact, Champagne is made from still wines; the bubbles are due to the fermentation of the natural grape sugar being halted until after the wine is bottled. In the bottle, the fermentation begins again and continues until the wine is drunk.

True Champagne is made in the region of that name in France. It is a blended wine, usually produced from two basic grape varietals – Pinot Noir (a red wine grape) and Chardonnay. Most Champagnes are nonvintage – that is, they are made from blended wines from several different years. It is the skill of the blender that differentiates one Champagne from another. If one vintage is thought to be particularly good, then a single vintage Champagne will be made and the bottle will bear the year on the label.

Some Champagnes are labelled Blanc de Blancs, which indicates that only white grapes were used to make them. These Champagnes are lighter and more delicate than standard blends. Another variation is the Crémant, which is less sparkling than a traditional Champagne.

Just before the final bottling, a sugar syrup is added to the wine. If very little syrup is added, the Champagne will be dry, and is labelled Brut. A little more syrup and it is Extra Sec. Sec is a bit sweeter, and Demi Sec sweeter still. Sweetest of all is Rich Champagne.

Sparkling wines are made elsewhere in France, but they are not called Champagne because, by law, the name is reserved for the wines of the Champagne region. (This is true throughout the EEC.) The other sparkling wines are called *mousseux*. The best of these are made by the *méthode champenoise*, in which fermentation takes place in the bottle as for true Champagne. The other method is called *cuve close*. For this, the second fermentation takes place in

A variety of bottle shapes from left: a green, high shouldered, Bordeaux bottle; a slope shouldered Burgundy bottle; the shorter, Côtes-du-Rhône bottle; a wide-based Provençal bottle; a slim, Alsace bottle; a shoulderless bottle, in green glass for Moselle wine, and brown glass for Rhine wine; a Champagne bottle is larger as it is made of thicker glass; clear glass is used for rosé Champagne

large sealed tanks, and the resulting wine is drawn off under pressure to be bottled. Both these methods are also used throughout the world. A third method, used only for the cheapest wines, is carbonation. Carbon dioxide gas is injected into tankfuls of still wine and the wine is bottled under pressure.

Spumante is the name given to the sparkling wines of Italy. The most famous is Asti Spumante, which is sweet and white. Other *spumantes* may be sweet or dry, red, rosé or white. German sparkling wine is called *sekt*. It is generally white, fruity and slightly sweet.

In the United States, sparkling wines – called champagne in the US, with the origin added as in 'Californian champagne' – are made in California and New York State. As with *mousseux*, the best are made using the *méthode champenoise*. American sparkling wines can range from dry to sweet.

Other countries produce sparkling wines; Spain (e.g. Cava), Portugal, Australia and the Soviet Union.

FORTIFIED WINES

Fortified wines are wines to which brandy (or white spirit made from distilled wine) has been added to increase the alcoholic content and, in some cases, arrest fermentation. The best-known fortified wines are sherry and port. Marsala, Madeira and Malaga are also well known. There are a number of other fortified aperitif wines and fruity *vins doux naturels* available.

Vermouth

Fortified with neutral alcohol, vermouth may be flavoured with as many as 30 to 40 different herbs, roots, berries, flowers and seeds. There are four basic varieties: extra dry white vermouth; sweet white, generally called bianco; red vermouth, which is usually sweet; and rosé vermouth. Both French and Italian versions of vermouth are available. Only the fine vermouth of Chambéry, flavoured with Alpine herbs, enjoys an *Appellation Contrôlée*.

Sherry

True sherry comes from the district around the town of Jerez de la Frontera in Southwest Spain. Here grapes may still be crushed in the traditional way, underfoot. The resulting juice is completely fermented before fortification, to produce dry wine, which is then stored in wooden casks in warehouses called *bodegas*. If a film of yeast cells, called a *flor*, develops on the surface of the wine, this will impart a unique flavour to the finished wine; such wines become the light, dry sherries called finos. Wines that do not develop a *flor* are destined to become olorosos – heavier, more perfumed sherries.

Sherries are made by the *solera* system, which involves blending wines of different ages and styles. For this reason, sherries are not labelled by vintage or individual vineyards – they take the name of the producer or house.

This popular wine can be very dry, medium, or very sweet and rich. A fino is a very dry, pale sherry. A manzanilla is the driest of all finos, and has an almost salty tang. A true amontillado is a fino that has been aged to produce a great depth of dry flavour and character; however, all but the most expensive amontillados today are just blended wines, sweetened to a 'medium' level. A true oloroso is dark gold in colour, dry, and aged to a nutty, smooth flavour. An oloroso becomes a dark, sweet cream sherry through the addition of sweetening and colouring in the final stages of blending.

Only sherry produced in the Jerez region can be so-called; all other sherry-type wines have to be labelled by their place of origin, as in Cyprus sherry, etc. Even the wine-producing region of Montilla, very near Jerez, cannot use the name sherry for its wines, even though they are similar to those of Jerez.

Sherry-type fortified wines are made throughout the world. Some producers use the traditional *flor* method and age their wines in small barrels; but many age the wines artificially by baking them in hot rooms.

Port

Port comes from vineyards along the Douro River in Northern Portugal, and it takes its name from Oporto, the city at the mouth of the Douro.

Port is made quite differently from sherry. The juice from the crushed grapes begins to ferment, but this is stopped prematurely by the addition of brandy. Because there is still a lot of unfermented sugar left, the resulting wine is both strong and sweet. The new wine is a deep purplish-red and very fruity; it changes colour and character during its ageing in wooden casks or in bottles, and it is the length of this ageing, and the environment in which it takes place, that determines the style of the finished wine.

Ruby ports are aged in wood for only a few years. They have a rich colour and fruity taste.

Tawny ports are a shade drier, and lighter in colour than ruby port, and these differences are primarily due to the fact that tawny ports are aged in wood for a longer period than ruby ports. The finest tawny ports are aged in casks for 10-40 years and as a result have a silkily smooth, mellow taste.

Occasionally the port shippers 'declare a vintage'; that is, they decide that a year's crop is good enough to produce wines that will last for well over 20 years, and up to 60 or 70 years. A vintage port is aged in wood for only 2-3 years before it is bottled. The further maturing in bottle takes place at a slower rate than in wood. The resulting wine is deep in colour, with a rich, intense flavour and a very heavy sediment.

'Late Bottled Vintage' and 'Vintage Character' ports form an increasingly popular category: they are, in effect, top quality ruby ports given four or five years in cask to speed the ageing process. These wines resemble the older vintage port, but without the same depth, and they are not intended to be matured in the bottle.

White port is made from white grapes. It is made in the same way as red port, and is made in both medium-sweet and full-bodied dry styles, the difference depending on the point at which brandy is added to the fermenting wine. Both versions make an excellent aperitif.

Madeira

This distinctive fortified wine takes its name from the Portuguese island where it is made. For sweet Madeira, the fermentation of the grape juice is stopped prematurely by the addition of brandy; dry Madeira, like sherry, is completely fermented before the brandy is added. The wines are then 'baked' for several months in rooms called *estufas*, or ovens. It is this baking process that gives Madeira its very special, elegantly balanced taste.

The driest Madeira is labelled Sercial and is made from grapes that are cousins to Germany's Riesling. Next in sweetness comes Verdelho, followed by Bual. The sweetest Madeira is Malmsey.

Fine vintage Madeiras are produced in addition to blended non-vintage wines. These are much rarer than Port vintages, and are not announced until 30 years after the vintage year itself. Even at this stage, they are still young wines, and when aged in bottles will go on developing layers of flavour almost indefinitely.

Marsala

Marsala comes from Sicily. It is completely fermented until dry, like sherry, and then fortified and, in some cases, sweetened to make a rich dark dessert wine. The very best Marsala is labelled *superiore* or *vergine*: the former can be either dry or sweet, while the latter is always dry. Some Marsalas are also flavoured with egg yolks (*all' uovo*), almonds and so on: these are known as *speciali*, and their quality is in general some way below the best that Sicily has to offer.

Malaga

A sweet, dark, raisin-flavoured fortified wine from Southern Spain. It was very popular in Victorian times.

The Wines of France

When the Romans came to France they found vineyards in Provence and Languedoc that had been there for centuries. The Romans extended the growing of grapes and took their wine-making skills with them up through the Rhône valley, across to Bordeaux, to Burgundy and the Loire, and on to Paris and Champagne. By the time they withdrew in the fifth century BC, almost all of the great French wine regions had been defined.

During the Dark Ages which followed the fall of the Roman Empire, the Church took over the vineyards. Monasteries became identified with wine, and for centuries the Church owned the greatest vineyards in Europe. The quality of the wine was much improved in this period.

Gradually, control of the vineyards passed from the Church into other hands. Many medieval monarchs took a great interest in making – and drinking – wine, and created a vogue for certain types. When Henry II of England married Eleanor of Aquitaine, she brought him the vineyards of her native duchy (which included what is now Bordeaux) as part of her dowry. As a result, claret – as the British call red Bordeaux – became very fashionable in England.

Today a French vineyard may be owned by one man or by a farmers' co-operative, and modern technology has helped the winemaker improve the quality of his wine considerably.

It has also helped him increase output, sometimes at the expense of quality. The bulk of the wine produced in France is ordinary everyday wine, or *vin ordinaire*. In fact, it is only about 10-15 per cent of each year's production of wine that can qualify as *Appellation Contrôlée* wine, and an even smaller fraction of that is 'fine wine' suitable for laying down. This general *Appellation Contrôlée* (or controlled naming) is strictly enforced, so you can be confident that the wine in the bottle was

PRODUCE OF FRANCE

PREMIERES CÔTES DE BORDEAUX

APPELLATION PREMIERES CÔTES DE
BORDEAUX CONTRÔLÉE

SELECTED
FOR
TESCO

Sweet White Wine

11.5% Vol

70 cl e

MIS EN BOUTEILLE PAR LES FILS DE MARCEL
QUANCARD LA GRAVE D'AMBARES GIRONDE

READING THE LABEL

French law protects the buyer: what you read on the label should define the quality spectrum of the wine in the bottle.

It is not traditional practice in France to mention the kind of grape that is used in a wine. This is because, by law, traditional grape varieties must be used if the wine is called by the traditional name. For example, for a wine to be called a white burgundy (or Bourgogne Blanc), it must be made entirely from Chardonnay grapes.

The wine-growing area must be mentioned on the label, and the quality of the wine can be judged

made in the area named.

The most unpredictable influence on wine is the weather, and it is this very unpredictability of the French climate that makes its fine wines so variable. The differing combinations of rain, sun, temperature and humidity are an important factor in defining the character of a wine; no two vintages are ever the same.

THE GREAT WINE REGIONS

Burgundy

Long before Christianity came to France, Burgundy was famous for its wine. Today the wines of this region tend to be unpredictable because many small holders, often amateur, cultivate their own vineyards on small plots of land. The result is that large quantities of very poor burgundy are produced every year; these, though, can command high prices on the basis of their famous names.

For this reason, it is best to learn the names of the good *négociants* and wine makers and to look for them on the labels. Some top burgundy *négociants* are Bouchard Père & Fils, Joseph Drouhin and Louis Jadot.

The three areas of Burgundy (Côte d'Or, Côte Chalonnaise and the Mâconnais) produce both red and white wines. In general the reds are rich in colour with an intense, medium-bodied taste. The whites tend to be straw gold, full and dry. Chablis, although not in Burgundy, is considered to be part of this wine region.

The great red wines of Burgundy

by how specific the designation is. In Burgundy, the vineyards are divided into four classes, and the wine must be labelled accordingly. At the bottom of the scale is the ordinary Bourgogne; next come the village wines (e.g. Gevrey-Chambertin, etc); *Premier Cru* labels give the name of the village followed by the name of the vineyard; the best, *Grand Cru*, simply give the name of their noble vineyard.

Appellation Contrôlée regulations cover more than the area and grape variety; they stipulate maximum quantities, minimum strengths, methods of pruning and a lot more. Similar, though less stringent, regulations govern the next grade of quality wine, VDQS (*Vin Delimité de Qualité Supérieure*), and the new third grade of *Vin de Pays*. The regulations governing ordinary table wine (*Vin de Table*) are, by comparison, lax.

After the wine has been aged in the cask, it may be bottled at source (*mis en bouteille à la propriété* or *au domaine*, or *mis en bouteille par le propriétaire*) or shipped to someone else to bottle. The name of the *négociant* (shipper) is often given on the label.

The labels of Bordeaux's fine wines will generally contain the words *mis en bouteille au château*: this guarantees that the wine was bottled at the château itself.

include Le Corton (one of the finest red burgundies), Volnay, Pommard, Côte de Beaune and Côte de Nuits St. George. Among the finest whites are the single vineyard wines of Montrachet and Corton-Charlemagne, as well as the village wines of Meursault and Chassagne-Montrachet and the wines of Chablis region.

Bordeaux
Generally acknowledged to be the greatest wine-producing region in France, Bordeaux is also the largest. There are five main areas, three of which produce red wine (Médoc, St. Emilion and Pomerol), one white (Sauternes) and one both red and white (Graves). The wines vary widely in character, but the region's fame lies in the good to superlative red wines of the Médoc, such as Château Lafite, Château Latour and Château Margaux and in the sweet, golden Sauternes, of which the finest is Château d'Yquem.

Each of the many famous châteaux in Bordeaux produces wine that has its own distinct characteristics. Even if the vineyards are side by side, the wine from one will consistently be different from the other. One reason for this is that wine in Bordeaux is made from a blend of two to four grape varieties (primarily Cabernet Sauvignon, Cabernet Franc and Merlot for red wine, and Sémillon and Sauvignon Blanc for white), and the proportions of each of these chosen by the wine maker decides the personality of the finished wine.

A bottle labelled Bordeaux Supérieur or Graves Supérieur does not imply better quality; it only means that the wine inside contains 1 or 2 per cent more alcohol than a bottle labelled simply Bordeaux or Graves.

Beaujolais
Many people think of the wines of this region as being cheap and cheerful: an antidote, in their *nouveau* form, to the gloom of mid-November. There is actually a wide variation in quality.

About 99 per cent of the wine made in the region is red, from the Gamay grape, and its main characteristics are freshness and fruitiness. The less expensive Beaujolais wines are intended to be drunk before they are 3 years old. This is because they are made by a process called carbonic maceration, which involves fermenting whole bunches of grapes, uncrushed, in sealed vats. The resulting wine is aromatic and fruity, but will not keep well.

Beaujolais-Villages is a step up from the basic Beaujolais, and it is a delicious wine. Above this are the *crus* of Beaujolais, the wines that take their names from the villages in which they are made: Moulin-à-Vent, Fleurie, Brouilly, Côte-de-Brouilly, Morgon, Saint-Amour, Chénas, Juliénas and Chiroubles. These lines have a richer, fuller taste and are longer-lived than the *villages* or ordinary Beaujolais.

Alsace
The wines of this region are fruity, with a fine, grapey bouquet. Riesling, Gewürztraminer, Pinot Gris (usually labelled Tokay d'Alsace) and Muscat are among the best white grapes of Alsace, and the wines they make beautifully complement the rich cooking of the region. All Alsace wines must, by law, be bottled in Alsace. Alsace is the only region in France to base its *Appellation Contrôlée* system on grape variety names.

Champagne
The name Champagne describes both the defined area in which the wine is made and the process it undergoes. As in Burgundy, there are thousands of local growers producing grapes that are then vinified and blended together. About one-third of the crop of the region is processed by the growers themselves, and is sold mainly in France. The remainder is sold to the famous houses in Reims and Epernay (see page 9).

Loire
Although the Loire River sees wide variations in climate and soil along its 960 km (600 miles), the wines of the

area are similar in that they are mainly light and fruity. The majority of Loire wines are white, both dry and sweet, with some red from Touraine and rosé from Anjou.

Muscadet, which is the name of a grape and not a place, is a popular dry white wine from the upper Loire. Further down the river is the home of the robustly aromatic Pouilly-Fumé and its partner across the river, Sancerre.

Rhône

This region has climate and soil conditions as varied as those of the Loire. The wines are mainly red and are a blend of anything from two to thirteen grape varieties. Côtes-du-Rhône is the general *appellation* given to red, white and rosé wines produced in the 150-odd parishes, or communes, to the north. Those wines made in the 14 superior communes in the southern part are called Côtes-du-Rhône-Villages.

Hermitage is one of the great Rhône wines. Other well-known Rhône wines are Côte-Rôtie and St-Joseph.

The Midi and Provence

In this huge region, much wine is produced but for the most part it is not of high quality. It is intended to be drunk young, and is cheap. Most of these wines are *Vins de Pays*, or simple *Vins de Table*; the better ones among them are VDQS or *Appellation Contrôlée*. Included among these are Côteaux du Languedoc (red), Corbières (red), Minervois (red), St. Chinian (red), Costières du Gard (red), and Côteaux d'Aix-en-Provence (white, rosé and red). Other notable *appellations* include Côtes du Roussillon (red), Fitou (red).

Southwest France

The wines made in this region are not fine or great, but many are of an excellent standard and offer good value. Amongst the most worthy of the red wine *appellations* are Cahors, Pécharmant, Côtes de Buzet and Madiran. For white wines, look for Monbazillac (sweet), Montravel and Jurançon, and for both red and white Côtes de Duras and Bergerac.

The Wines of Italy

Wines have been grown throughout Italy for almost 3,000 years. Today, Italy's annual production of wine is greater than that of any other country, including France. The best wines of Italy can be every bit as good as the fine wines of France and Germany.

Italian wine names

The same wine names – Chianti, Barolo, Soave and so on – are used for wines of varying quality as well as style (for example, Orvieto can be sweet or dry). Wine names can refer to the town or village of origin (such as Orvieto), the region (such as Chianti), the grape (such as Verdicchio), or something completely fantastical like Lacryma Christi (the Tears of Christ). In 1963, the Italian government introduced laws defining the major wine regions and controlling wine labelling along the lines of those enforced in France and Ger-

many, and these have cleared up some of the confusion.

Before the government stepped in, the growers and shippers in several wine-producing districts formed committees, or *consorzio*, to set certain minimum standards for their wine. Not all the growers or shippers in the area joined these *consorzio*, but those who did generally indicate this by a small neck label featuring the symbol of the consorzio concerned.

THE WINE REGIONS

Tuscany

This region, with Florence as its capital, produces one of the most famous red wines in the world – Chianti. In fact, only about one-quarter of Tuscan wines are Chianti, and of that only 15 per cent are given the designation Chianti Classico. The neck labels of this wine bear the

---

READING THE LABEL

The Government designation *Denominazione di Origine Controllata* indicates that the wine has been produced in a specific region, and that it meets set standards of quality as regards grapes used, methods of production, limited yields and proper ageing. By law, this DOC can be used by only about 200 wines; however, they vary greatly in quality. The next rung up, *Denominazione di Origine Controllata e Garantita*, is a more reliable guide as it requires that even stricter conditions be met, and only about five wines have, as yet, been given this honour by the government.

Here are some of the words found on Italian wine labels, together with an account of what they mean.

Classico, as in Chianti Classico, is added to the name of the region (here Chianti) when the wine comes from the centre and best part of that region. It is usually an indication of superior quality.

Riserva indicates that the wine was matured for longer than usual before bottling.

Superiore, like the French *supérieur,* means the wine has a higher alcoholic content, though it may not necessarily taste better.

The style of wine will be indicated on the label: *secco* is dry; *amabile* or *abboccato* is medium dry to medium sweet; *dolce* is sweet; *frizzante* is semi-sparkling; and *spumante* is fully sparkling.

Gallo Nero, a black cockerel on a gold background inside a red ring. Ordinary Chianti can be thin and bitter, so look for words on the label such as *Riserva* that denote quality. At its best, it is an excellent medium-bodied dry wine.

The traditional Chianti bottle is flask-shaped, set in a straw basket. It is obvious that these bottles were not designed to be laid on their sides, for further maturing, so any wine thus presented is intended to be drunk young. In fact, these *fiaschi* are being replaced by Bordeaux-style bottles, especially for Chianti Classico.

Umbria

The best known wine of the Umbria region (called 'the green heart of Italy') is Orvieto. A white wine, Orvieto is available in medium-dry versions (*abboccato*) as well as dry (*secco*).

Veneto

From around the city of Verona come the well-known wines Soave, Valpolicella and Bardolino. Soave is a light, crisp, dry white wine that is best drunk young. The other two wines are fresh, light-bodied reds that are equally re-freshing. An unusual wine from this region is Recioto. This is made from specially selected grapes that are dried and then fermented. It may be sweet (when it will be called Recioto di Valpolicella) or dry (when it will be called Amarone). It will be very strong, and is generally red.

Piedmont

Many of the best red wines of Italy come from this region. The finest of these is Barolo, made in and around the village of that name, from the Nebbiolo grape. Two other villages producing excellent red wines are Barbaresco and Gattinara. All of these wines are made to last, and benefit from several years maturing in bottle. Other red wines of the region are labelled according to the grape variety used, for example Nebbiolo, Barbera and Dolcetto. They vary in style from light and fruity (Dolcetto) to more astringent and concentrated in flavour (Nebbiolo and Barbera).

White wines are made from the Cortese grape and are often labelled as such. Gavi is one from this region.

Central and Southern Italy

In this large area, many popular white wines are produced, for example light, dry Verdicchio, from vineyards south of Ancona on the Adriatic Coast, and grapey Frascati, from Latium. Excellent red table wines are produced further south, particularly in Sicily.

Other Areas

Near Bologna, the capital of Emilia-Romagna, Lambrusco is made from the grape of that name. Available in dry or slightly sweet versions, as well as red or white, it usually has a slight sparkle.

In the northern Alto Adige region a wide number of red and white grape varieties, including Schiava, Chardonnay and Traminer, are grown to make light, flavourful white wines. Cabernet grapes are grown in Friuli-Venezia Giulia, in northeast Italy, to make good red wines; Pinot Grigio, Tocai and Verduzzo are three of the best white wines from the region.

The Wines of Germany

Despite the fact that the annual wine production of Germany is relatively small – only about one per cent of the world's total – it produces wines that are acknowledged to be among the finest in the world. The Germans themselves reserve their best and sweetest wines to be savoured alone, not as an accompaniment to food – a tip worth remembering.

The Riesling is the noble grape of Germany, and it produces superb white wines that have a distinctive flowery bouquet when young. Silvaner, Müller-Thurgau and Rülander are among the other German white grape varieties. Some German white wines are drier than others: look for the terms *Trocken* (dry) or *Halbtrocken* (medium dry) on the label. A few light red wines are made in Germany, too, but they represent only about 10 per cent of the annual production.

As in many other European wine-making countries, there are many thousands of growers in Germany who have only about four acres or less each; less than one per cent of all growers own more than 20 acres.

The vineyards are on steep hillsides along the banks of the Rhine and its many tributaries. Because some of these vineyards lie far north, where winters can be very cold and summers relatively cool, the vines are planted facing south. The steep incline of some of the vineyards makes it virtually impossible to use machinery, and the vines have to be tended by hand.

In Germany the weather is the single most important factor in wine-making. Unlike the rest of the world, where a good vintage is one in which the grapes ripen fully and healthily and the grape juice ferments completely to make a dry wine, in Germany the best vintages are ones in which the grapes are able to over-ripen and rot so that the resulting wine can be rich and sweet. A lack of sunshine will result in a harvest of grapes that are low in natural sugar and too acid to make an agreeable wine, so the producer must add unfermented grape juice (called *süssreserve*) to the wine before bottling to ensure the necessary degree of balance and sweetness.

The Connoisseur's Wines

Every year, in every German wine-producing community, the village council decrees the exact date of the harvest – the time by which the grapes should have achieved the minimum degree of ripeness – and no one may pick his grapes before that date. In certain years, some growers decide to wait one week or more after the official date before picking, so that the grapes can ripen more fully. In this case, the resulting wine is known as *Spätlese*, or late picked. Such a wine will be fuller-bodied, richer and sweeter than the rest of the wine from the vineyard. If the ripest bunches of grapes are separated from the rest, to be pressed and fer-

READING THE LABEL

German wine labels are very informative. They tell you about the ripeness of the grape, and they almost always give the exact place of origin as well as the vintage and conditions under which the grapes were picked. The grape variety is not always on the label because, for example, it is taken for granted that everyone will know all good vineyards in the Moselle and Rheingau grow only Riesling grapes. On the other hand, the best vineyards in the Rheinhessen and Rheinpfalz always label their Riesling wines accordingly because most of the grapes grown there are Silvaner and Müller-Thurgau.

There are four basic categories of wine quality: *Deutscher Tafelwein*, or table wine from German vineyards only; *Landwein*, roughly equivalent to the French *Vin de Pays*, usually rather drier than most German wines; *Qualitätswein bestimmten Anbaugebietes* (or QbA) which comes from one of the 11 quality wine regions and which represents the next quality platform; and finally *Qualitätswein mit Prädikat* (QmP), quality wine with a 'predicate' added, such as *Spätlese* or *Auslese*. Another predicate is *Kabinett*, used to designate basic QmP wines below the level of *Spätlese*, but with no sugar added to them during fermentation.

The word *Erzeugerabfüllung* tells you that the wine was bottled by the grower.

mented on their own, the wine made is called *Auslese*. It will be richer – and more expensive – than a *Spätlese*.

A further refinement is to put aside especially ripe individual grapes to make a sweet and fragrant wine from them called *Beerenauslese*. Naturally, such wines are scarce, and higher in price than an *Auslese*, but still less than a *Trockenbeerenauslese*, the top of this wine hierarchy. This rare wine – very sweet yet not cloying – is made from overripe, shrivelled grapes that have a very high natural sugar content. All of these names are legally defined according to the percentage of sugar in the unfermented must.

There is one other rare German wine. This is *Eiswein*, or ice wine, which is made from fully ripe grapes, of at least *Spätlese* quality, that have frozen on the vine. To make this, the grower must wait patiently until the winter frosts arrive.

MAJOR WINE REGIONS

Rheingau: superb, rich, fragrant wines the best of which will keep and improve over a period of twenty or more years.

Mosel-Saar-Ruwer: refreshing, light wines, pale in colour with green glints; the most delicate in flavour and balance of all German wines.

Rheinhessen: mellow, agreeable wines made from a variety of grapes.

Rheinpfalz (Rhenish Palatinate): soft, full, rounded wines often with a spicy element in their flavour.

Nahe: fresh, full-flavoured wines: often good quality/price ratio.

Baden: large area of wines of variable quality; many red wines.

Franconia: drier wines than those of the rest of Germany with more body and a distinct earthy taste. Bottled in distinctive, squat 'bocksbeutel' bottles.

WINES

The Wines of Spain and Portugal

A tremendous amount of wine is made in Spain, only 3 per cent of which is sherry. The best are the fine red wines of the Rioja district in the north. The Portuguese are also great wine-makers: only 2 per cent of the annual Portuguese wine production is port; the rest is made up of agreeable red, white and rosé wines.

READING THE LABEL

Reserva **indicates that the wine has been specially selected to be aged in wood longer than usual, and should be of a superior quality.** *Gran reserva* **has been aged for still longer before being bottled and released onto the market, and these words on a label should indicate a very fine wine. (The number of years (*año*) that the wine was kept in wood will sometimes be given.)**

The following Spanish terms are used to describe styles of wine: *vino de mesa* **or** *de pasto* **(table wine);** *blanco* **(white);** *rosado* **(rosé);** *clarete* **(light red or dark rosé);** *tinto* **(red);** *seco* **(dry);** *abocado* **or** *dulce* **(sweet); and** *espumoso* **(sparkling).**

In Portugal, the words *Denominação de Origem* **on the label are equivalent to the Spanish DO, and the term** *Reserva* **is used in the same way. A very good quality wine is indicated by the designation** *Garrafeira*; **this wine will have been aged by the producer before being released onto the market, and many are suitable for further ageing.**

Words to watch out for on Portuguese labels include *tinto* **(red),** *branco* **(white) and** *verde* **(meaning green, but is used to imply young).**

The governments of both Spain and Portugal have already introduced wine laws similar to the French *Appellation Contrôlée* laws. *Denominación de Origen* is the Spanish equivalent, and is given to those regions producing ordinary wine intended for bulk shipping and blending out of the country as well as to the better wine regions.

A vintage (*vendimia* or *cosecha*) may be given, but this doesn't necessarily mean that the wine in the bottle was made solely from grapes harvested the same year. This is because the climate of Spain is so dependable, making each year's crop much the same, and wines of several vintages are often blended together, thus ensuring consistency of style in a company's wines.

Many Portuguese table wines are sold under a brand name, or the name of the producer, rather than the name of the grape or region. Two exceptions are the Dão and Bairrada regions, noted for their excellent earthy red wines.

SPANISH WINE REGIONS

Rioja
In this large mountainous region not far from the French border, wine has been made for a very long time, and the methods of production are similar to those traditionally used in Bordeaux. One reason for this is that a number of French wine-making families moved across the Pyrenees to Rioja about 100 years ago, bringing their vinification techniques with them.

The wines of Rioja are rich in tannin with a deep colour. Their hallmark is the strong aroma of vanilla they possess, the result of being aged in oak. There are three main grades of Rioja: *Vino de Crianza*, *Reserva* and *Gran Reserva*, and these relate to how long the wines have been aged in casks, *Gran Reserva* being the oldest and finest. (You will see these names on the DO label on

Penedès
This small hilly region behind the Costa Dorada produces both sparkling and still wines, reds, whites and rosés. The best-known producer is Torres, whose wines consistently win awards in international competitions.

Other regions
Navarra, just to the north of Rioja, produces light red and white wines of increasingly high quality. La Mancha, the Don Quixote country of Central Spain, produces much table wine: Valdepeñas is the demarcated area within La Mancha where the best red wines are produced.

Jumilla, inland from Alicante, produces easy-drinking, full-bodied red wines.

In Ribeiro and Valdeorras, just across the border from Portugal, young, fresh white wines and bigger, firmly structured red wines are produced.

the back of the bottle.) White Rioja is also made, and can be as good as its red counterpart. There are two styles: the full-bodied traditional, aged in oak, and the 'new' style of crisp, fresh wines.

Most of the vineyards are small, each owned by one of hundreds of farmers who sell their grapes to a winery (*bodega*), co-operative cellar or shipper for blending. Because Rioja is a blended wine, there are almost no famous vineyards in this region. Instead, each producer sells his wine under a number of brand names.

The three districts within this region are Rioja Alta, Rioja Baja and Rioja Alavesa.

PORTUGUESE WINE REGIONS

Dão
Both red and white wines are made in this extensive region in the central part of Portugal. The better reds certainly deserve ageing, so that their full meaty flavour can be allowed to develop and mellow. White Dão is also produced, and its quality is rapidly improving.

Bairrada
The red wines of Bairrada are well-worth seeking out: they are higher in fruit and fragrance than those of Dão.

Minho
Vinho verde is produced in this province north of the Douro River. This 'green' wine can, in fact, be red or white (although only the whites are exported); the name refers not to the colour of the wine but to its youthfulness. The wine is bottled early, within a few months of the vintage, so that a second fermentation takes place in the bottle, giving the resulting wine a slight sparkle.

Other popular Portuguese sparkling wines are available in both rosé and white versions.

The Wines of the New World

The United States

Most of the wine produced in the United States comes from vineyards on the East and West coasts, and the major wine-making state is California. Californian wine ranges in quality from ordinary table wine to outstanding, very fine wine, and it may be red, white, rosé or sparkling. Fortified wines (called dessert wines there) are also made.

The first vines were planted in California about 200 years ago, by Spanish missionaries. In the 1850s, cuttings of many more European vines were brought to California, thus increasing the grape varieties available to the wine-makers, themselves mostly European immigrants. The flourishing wine trade they began was crippled by Prohibition, and the industry had to start again almost from scratch when Prohibition was repealed.

Californian wine may be labelled with a generic name (i.e. as the Californian version of a famous European wine name such as Burgundy or Chablis) or with a varietal name (i.e. labelled according to the grape variety primarily used to make the wine). Generically labelled wines are very rarely exported. Most Californian wines seen here are varietal wines, made from classic European grape varieties.

When a bottle of Californian wine states a grape variety on the label, at least 75 per cent (and often more) of the wine inside will have been made from that variety. California's most successful varietal wines are those made from Cabernet Sauvignon (for red wines) and Chardonnay (for white wines), and these are nearly always excellent value for money. California's native grape Zinfandel also makes exciting fruity red wines, and Merlot is another red variety producing increasingly impressive wines. All of these can be very fine indeed, and many of the best come from the San Francisco area, from wineries in the counties of Sonoma, Napa and Santa Cruz. It should be remembered, though, that as the wine industry in California is so young – and so energetic – many new areas are still being explored, and it will be decades before California's regions have the precise identity that those of France have enjoyed for centuries.

One might think that because the weather in California is so dependable, allowing the grapes to ripen fully before harvesting, there is no difference between one vintage and another. In fact, this is not always the case, particularly around San Francisco where there is a great range of climatic conditions.

All information on Californian wine labels is strictly controlled by state and federal law. If a label gives a vintage, it means that the wine inside was made 100 per cent from grapes harvested and pressed that year. If the geographical origin of the wine is given, 75 per cent of the grapes used must have come from the named district or state. If the wine is 'produced and bottled by' someone, 75 per cent of the wine must have been made at that winery; 'estate-bottled' indicates that all the wine was produced at the winery from grapes grown on its own property.

Elsewhere in the United States, wine is made in Oregon, Washington State, Idaho, Michigan, Virginia, Maryland, Missouri, Pennsylvania, Arkansas, Texas, Ohio and New York State. Many states produce wines mainly from native American grapes, such as Catawba and Concorde; these have a pungent aroma and distinctive 'foxy' flavour.

Australia

The wine-making industry started on a large scale in Australia in the 1830s, and at the outset produced far more fortified wine than table wine. Today, however, the production of table wine is steadily increasing.

As in California, cuttings of classic European grape varieties were taken to Australia to start their vineyards. These were planted in widely disparate areas, ranging from the Hunter River Valley in New South Wales to the Barossa Valley in Victoria (nearly 800 miles from the Hunter River Valley), or from Coonawarra in the south to Perth on the western coast of the continent.

Australian wines are sometimes said to be similar in character and style to Californian wines. Both California and Australia are very fortunate in comparison with Europe in the amount of sunshine they enjoy; unlike Europe, the problems they face are in general connected with lack of rainfall. For this reason, the emphasis in recent years (particularly in Australia) has been on finding 'cool-climate' areas (like Mount Helen in central Victoria) in which to grow grapes: this has resulted in Australian wines of increasing subtlety and delicacy.

As in California, many of the best wines are those made from named grape varieties. Among those of particular note are Shiraz (similar to the Rhône's Syrah), Cabernet Sauvignon, Grenache and Pinot Noir for red wines, and Semillon, Rhine Riesling, Chardonnay, Sauvignon Blanc and Gewürztraminer for whites. The red wines range from the massively full-bodied (certain Shiraz wines) to the light and fruity (Grenache and blended wines). Australian white wines may be light and fragrant with a fruity flavour (Rhine Riesling) or soft and full-bodied (Chardonnay and Semillon). Excellent Muscats are also produced in Australia, both dry and dessert.

Well-known producers are Brown Brothers, Château Tahbilk, Mildara, The Rothbury Estate, Penfold's, Tyrell's and Wynn's. Fine Australian wines, unlike those of Europe, are generally designed to be drunk as soon as they are released on to the market, rather than being stored for maturation in a cellar over a period of years. If your storage space is limited, the better quality Australian wines are well-worth trying.

New Zealand

Most of the wine produced in New Zealand is still destined for domestic consumption, although year by year exports are increasing. The vineyards, found in Blenheim in the north of the South Island, and around Auckland and Hawke's Bay on the North Island, are planted mainly with white wine grapes. The most important of these is Müller-Thurgau, though Chardonnay, Gewürztraminer, Sauvingon Blanc and Chenin Blanc are also of increasing importance. These white wines are usually medium dry and fruity with a flowery aroma.

Some red wines are also made, primarily from the Cabernet Sauvignon grape, though Pinot Noir (the grape variety used in France to make red burgundy) is also producing some very promising wines. Of all the New World regions, New Zealand has the coolest and most temperate climate, and as this factor is thought nowadays to be critical in producing wines of Old World subtlety and finesse, the country's wine-making future is being watched with eager attention.

The Wines from the rest of the World

Greece

The Ancient Greeks were great makers and drinkers of wine. Today Greece continues to produce a variety of robustly flavoured wines in large quantities.

About half of the Greek table wines – mostly white – are flavoured, during fermentation, with a small amount of pine resin. This gives Retsina (as this wine is called) an unusual and haunting flavour that complements the rich, olive oil-based dishes of Greek cuisine. Non-resinated red and white wines are also made. The most famous Greek dessert wines are the rich and sweet red Mavrodaphne and the sweet white Samos.

Cyprus

Cyprus is, of course, best known for its sherry – but it does produce wines very similar to those of Greece. The main producers are Keo and Sodap. Robust red wines account for around 75 per cent of its total production. It also produces a fine quality sweet dessert wine called Commandaria.

EASTERN EUROPE

Hungary: Wine has been in Hungary for a very long time. Tokay is Hungary's classic white wine, and it may be a dry aperitif wine (Tokay Szamorodni), a medium dry table wine (Tokay Furmint), or a lusciously sweet dessert wine (Tokay Aszu). The more ordinary wines of the country include the popular Bull's Blood (*Egri Bikaver* in Hungarian): a full-bodied, hearty, dry red wine.

Bulgaria: Wine has been made commercially here for only about 35 years, but Bulgaria is now one of the world's top wine exporters. The wines are labelled according to grape variety, and the best are the fruity red Cabernet Sauvignons and white Chardonnays. Quality levels are consistent, and the wines are excellent value for money.

Yugoslavia: Yugoslavia produces a lot of inexpensive red and white table wines, as well as dessert wines. The best-known come from the northern province of Slovenia, from vineyards around the cities of Lutomer, Maribor, Ormoz and Radgona.

NORTH AFRICA

A small wine trade in Algeria, Morocco and Tunisia is producing some top quality wines. Of particular note are their dark, full-bodied reds.

SOUTH AMERICA

Chile and Argentina are the leading wine-making countries of Latin America.

The best grape-growing area in Chile is around Santiago. There the vineyards are planted with classic French grape varieties – Cabernet Sauvignon, Merlot, Pinot Noir, Sauvignon Blanc, Sémillon and the Rhine Riesling – and the wine made can be of excellent quality. Varietal names are used to label the wines, which are good value.

Most of the vast quantity of wine produced in Argentina is inexpensive table wine, for local consumption. That which is exported is mostly rather heavy wine, mainly red, but some better quality wines are appearing in Britain.

ENGLAND

Most of the wine is white, from newly-developed German grape varieties, and it is light, delicate and fruity with a flowery hedgerow bouquet. As might be expected, chaptalization (the addition of sugar to the fermenting grape juice) is usually necessary to create sound, agreeable wines. Unfortunately, English wine is expensive because it is produced in such small quantities and under difficult climatic conditions.

24

Wine Vintages

FRANCE	1976	77	78	79	80	81	82	83	84	85
Bordeaux	2	1	3	2	1	2	3	3	1	3
Sauternes	3	1	1	2	2	2	1	3	1	2
Red Burgundy	2	1	3	2	1	2	2	3	2	3
White Burgundy	1	1	3	2	2	3	2	3	2	3
Loire	3	1	3	1	1	2	3	2	2	2
Northern Rhône	3	1	3	2	2	1	3	3	1	3
Southern Rhône	2	2	3	2	2	2	1	2	2	3
Alsace	3	1	2	2	1	2	2	3	2	2
GERMANY										
Mosel-Saar-Ruwer	3	1	1	3	2	2	2	3	1	2
Rheingau	3	1	2	2	1	2	1	3	1	3
Rheinpfalz	3	1	1	2	2	2	1	3	1	2
Nahe	3	1	1	2	2	2	1	3	1	2
Rheinhessen	3	1	1	3	1	2	1	2	2	2
ITALY										
Piedmont	2	1	3	3	2	1	3	3	1	3
Tuscany	1	2	2	2	2	2	3	2	1	3
Veneto	2	2	2	2	1	1	2	3	1	3
PORTUGAL										
Port	–	3	1	–	2	–	2	2	–	–
SPAIN										
Rioja	2	1	3	1	2	2	3	2	1	3

3 good to excellent   – no port vintage declared
2 average to good
1 poor to average   Note: All 1985 ratings are provisional

How to use the vintage chart

The vintage chart above provides a rough guide to the relative importance of vintages in Europe's main wine-growing regions. (Vintages in other parts of the world are, as a rule, more consistent from year to year than are those of Europe.)

Although a rating has been given for every region listed, certain regions consistently produce wines of greater longevity than others: Bordeaux, Sauternes, Burgundy, the Rhône, Piedmont, Rioja and the Douro Valley's vintage ports. Middle and top quality wines from these regions should go on improving steadily over a period of 10 years, providing the vintages have been graded 2 or **3**.

For other regions, and in particular the Loire, Veneto, and all regions of Germany, only choose vintages more than 5 years old when you can be assured that the wines are of top quality, and the vintages have been graded **3**.

Buying, Storing and Serving Wine

In every shop that sells wine – be it supermarket, off-licence or speciality wine merchant – there is a bewildering variety of wines available, from many countries and at widely differing prices. There is also a choice of wine in familiar – and exotic and unfamiliar – bottles, in boxes with taps for serving, in soft-drink cans and in cartons like fruit juice.

Wines in bottles: The 'standard' wine bottle varies greatly in size – from 70 cl to 75 cl in Europe – and wine can also be bought in half bottles and those that contain 1 litre, 1.5 litres (a magnum), 2 and even 3 litres. Legislation has now been introduced to help the consumer; in most countries, the capacity of the bottle must be given on it. Also, in January 1989 all the wine-making countries in the EEC will have to use a standard 75 cl bottle, as is normal in the United States and Australia.

Wine bottles are usually made of tinted glass to keep out the light. Inexpensive wines may have a screwcap, but finer wines are always stopped with a cork. The reason for this is that during ageing the wine must be allowed to 'breathe', both through the sides of the wooden casks before bottling and then – to a lesser extent – through the cork in the bottle.

It is worth noting here that too much air entering the bottle can eventually spoil the wine, so good bottles are generally stored lying on their sides, thus allowing the wine to keep the cork moist and expanded.

If an opened bottle of wine is not finished, it can be kept. Pour the wine into a smaller container, to remove as much air as possible, seal it, and keep it in the refrigerator. Full-bodied red wines will be fine for several days; fortified wines will stay in reasonable condition for 2 months, with the exception of fino or manzanilla sherry (best consumed within 2 weeks); even Champagne will keep its fizz for 1-2 days if tightly stoppered with a special seal. Leftover wine from cans and cartons can be stored in the same way.

Wine boxes: As might be expected, the wine box first made an appearance in Australia and California, where the lifestyle is relaxed and informal, reflecting the marvellously sunny climate. For picnics, barbecues or any other outdoor occasion where wine is to be served, the wine box is ideal.

The wine is packed in a laminated plastic balloon, which is encased in a cardboard box. The box is fitted with a special tap that prevents air getting back into the wine and spoiling it. As the wine is consumed, the balloon gradually deflates inside the box.

Wine boxes usually contain 3 litres (or more) of quite drinkable wine, and they can be considered good value for

money when compared to similar wine in bottles because of the convenience in the style of packaging.

Once a wine box is opened, the contents should last for between 3 weeks and 3 months.

Wine cartons: These containers look like fruit juice cartons. Just as for juice, you snip off the corner and pour out the wine into glasses or a jug. The cartons contain 500 ml or 1 litre; there are also mini-cartons that hold an individual serving. They are good value as the packaging is cheaper than glass.

Wine cans: Like the wine box, these cans – each containing one or two servings – are very convenient for informal wine-drinking occasions, particularly outdoors.

Where to buy

Where you buy wine can greatly affect the variety you will have to choose from and the price you pay.

Buying wine in supermarkets has increased dramatically in the past few years, and much more than just the well-known brands is now offered for sale. You can usually find wines from all over the world, at all quality levels and prices. An added advantage to buying wine in supermarkets is that you need not make a special trip for the purpose, and you can choose a bottle to complement the food you're going to cook (see pages 30-1).

The bigger off-licence chains are often very well stocked, with competitive prices. Many sell their own house brands which can be good value.

Wine merchants and shops are always happy to sell wines by the case, and a discount is usually given for this kind of purchase. Wine warehouses only sell wine by the case – though you can select 12 different bottles to make up your case. Low overheads mean that warehouses can offer very competitive prices.

As the buying power of supermarkets is unrivalled, their own brand wines are nearly always the best value available within any particular *appellation* or wine grouping.

A selection of containers available from most supermarkets. From left: a 1½ litre bottle; a 1 litre bottle; a 1 litre carton of red wine; a small ¼ litre carton, ideal for one or two glasses of wine; a 1 litre carton of white wine; a 3 litre box fitted with a special tap; a carton containing 70 cl of wine; cans of red and white wine; a re-usable carafe-style bottle containing red wine

Storing and keeping wine

If you intend to stock up with wine try to find a place in your home that you can use as a wine 'cellar'. This need not be a real cellar, of course – often in old houses the cellar is where the boiler is located, which makes for too variable a temperature.

In choosing the place for your wine cellar, there are just four simple rules to follow: ideally, wine should be kept between 8 and 13°C (45 and 55°F), although up to 21°C (70°F) is not disastrous – it just means the wine will mature more quickly; the temperature must be constant; the wine should be kept away from direct exposure to daylight and vibrations; and wine bottles should be stored on their sides, so that the corks are kept moist. A broom cupboard might meet all these conditions: you could then fit it with wine racks.

Having prepared the cellar, you now need to stock it with wine. This could be a mixture of the bottles you intend to consume relatively quickly – and to restock – as well as those fine wines you want to 'lay down' to mature.

Much of the fine wine sold today is not ready to drink, and it needs some time in bottle to develop its qualities. A young wine of this kind will prove to be quite a bargain when its purchase price is compared with its price when offered for sale at its prime. Many of these wines are available from good supermarkets and we have given some suggestions below. Traditional wine merchants can also help in the purchase of fine wines.

The following red wines are worth buying for laying down: fine claret, red burgundy from the best vineyards, fine Rhône wines such as Hermitage, Côte-Rôtie or Cornas, good Italian reds such as Barolo and Barbaresco, and Cabernet Sauvignons from the best Californian and Australian vineyards. White wines for laying down include the great Sauternes, great German sweet wines, good quality white burgundy and fine white Riojas. Finally, vintage port needs to be laid down for an absolute minimum of 10 years before drinking.

Serving wine

A great deal is written and said about the proper way to serve wine – and too much snobbery is attached to it. Basically, it is very straightforward and commonsensical.

Large tulip-shaped glasses, with a slight tapering-in towards the top, should be used – clear glass so that the colour of the wine can be appreciated, and stemmed so that the heat of your hand won't affect the temperature of the wine – and the glasses should be only half filled so that the wine can be gently swirled around before drinking. This swirling allows you to enjoy the smell of the wine as well as taste it.

Temperature: White wines, rosés and sparkling wines are best served chilled because they are meant to be refreshing. They mustn't be overchilled, however, because the colder a wine is, the less flavour it has. About 1-1½ hours in the refrigerator is sufficient; for faster chilling, immerse the bottle up to its neck in iced water for 15-20 minutes.

Some light red wines, such as Beaujolais and Valpolicella, benefit from a brief chilling, too – say 20 minutes in the refrigerator.

Red wines are meant to be served at

A wine rack showing how bottles can be stored on their sides

Decanting a bottle of red wine against a candle so the sediment is clearly visible

a cool room temperature, of about 15-18°C (60-65°F). In fact, as the modern wine cellar is likely to be just a cool cupboard, the wine is probably stored at or near this temperature. It is best to avoid serving wine at over 20°C (68°F) because no wine will then taste as good as it should.

Should a bottle be very cold, don't try to warm it up quickly by standing it in front of a fire or in the oven. This will only kill off its flavour and bouquet. Let it warm up as gradually as possible.

Sediment: Older red wines – and some white – may have developed a deposit or sediment, that (although completely harmless) is not particularly pleasant to drink. To deal with this, the bottle (which will generally have been stored lying on its side) should be stood upright for 1-2 hours before serving, to allow the sediment to settle on the bottom. When the wine is poured, be careful to leave the sediment in the bottle.

Another means of removing sediment is to decant the wine (see above).

Opening the bottle: A good corkscrew is an essential item of equipment for the wine-drinker. There are many different kinds; choose one that is simple, sturdy and efficient (like the Screwpull or Waiter's Friend types). Take all the foil

off the top of the bottle and wipe the top before inserting the corkscrew. If you crumble the cork into the wine, simply strain the wine – through a tea strainer or piece of clean muslin – into a clean container. If you break the cork, reinsert the corkscrew at an angle to get a good grip on the remaining piece.

Breathing and decanting: Some people believe a bottle of red wine should be opened at least 1 hour before serving, to allow it to 'breathe', or have some prolonged exposure to the air. This breathing is said to develop and release the flavour and bouquet, and to remove any harshness.

In fact, merely removing the cork is not enough. It is necessary to 'aerate' the wine by pouring it into a decanter and leaving it for a time before drinking.

If the wine does have a sediment, pour it slowly and steadily from the bottle into its new container against a strong light (traditionally a candle) so you can see the sediment clearly. When the sediment begins to reach the neck of the bottle, stop pouring immediately (see illustration above). Young wines benefit from this aeration as much as older, finer wines.

Wine and Food

FOOD	WINE
Pâté	strong white such as Gewürztraminer or Chardonnay, or dry rosé, or light red such as Beaujolais and Valpolicella
Consommé	dry sherry
Pizza	light or medium red such as Chianti, Barbera and Rioja
Pasta, with creamy sauce	dry crisp white such as Soave or Frascati
Pasta, with meat sauce	medium red such as Dolcetto or Nebbiolo
FISH	
Simple white fish dishes	light dry white such as Chablis, Pouilly-Fuissé and Muscadet or fruity white from the Moselle
Fish in rich creamy sauce	full-bodied white such as white burgundy, Rioja and Mâcon
Shellfish	light dry white such as Chablis, Muscadet, Soave and Pinot Grigio
Smoked fish	full-bodied white such as burgundy
Fish soup	dry Sercial Madeira
RED MEAT	
Beef, roasted or grilled	medium-bodied red such as burgundy, claret and Californian Zinfandel
Beef, in rich stew	hearty red such as Rhône, Barolo and Dāo
Lamb	light or medium-bodied red such as Beaujolais, Mâcon, Médoc, Chianti, Valpolicella and Zinfandel
Game birds	light or medium-bodied red such as claret, Beaujolais, Rioja and Chianti
Venison	full-bodied red such as Côtes-du-Rhône, burgundy, Californian Cabernet Sauvignon and Australian Shiraz
WHITE MEAT	
Pork	light or medium-bodied red such as Beaujolais and Chianti, or rosé, or medium-bodied dry white such as dry Orvieto, Graves and white burgundy

FOOD	WINE
Veal	full-bodied dry white such as Chardonnay, white burgundy and Riesling, or light red such as Beaujolais, Valpolicella and Californian Zinfandel
Ham	dry white such as Chardonnay and Sémillon, or dry rosé, or light red
Offal	light or medium-bodied red such as claret
POULTRY	
Chicken	medium-bodied dry white such as white burgundy, or rosé or light red (especially if roasted or cooked in red wine)
Duck	full-bodied white such as white burgundy, or rosé, or light red like Beaujolais or fuller red such as claret
Turkey	spicy white such as Gewürztraminer, or dry rosé, or light red
Goose	rich white such as German Spätlese or light red burgundy
CHEESE	
Soft (Brie, Camembert, etc.)	medium-bodied red such as red burgundy, claret, Rioja and Rhône
Cream or goat	medium-bodied white such as Graves
Medium (Cheddar, etc.)	light fruity red (Beaujolais or Chinon), or spicy white (Gewürztraminer), or medium red Dāo, or full-bodied red such as Barolo – depending on how mature the cheese is
Blue	light or medium-bodied red such as claret and Barbera, or ruby or tawny port
DESSERTS	
Fresh fruit	light fruity red or white dessert wine
Light dessert	dessert wine such as Muscat de Beaumes de Venise and German Auslese or Beerenauslese
Creamy dessert	rich dessert wine such as Tokay Aszu or Sauternes

Which wine to serve with which food is thought to be a difficult decision to make, but it really isn't. It's obvious that the established customs about this – red wine with red meat dishes and white wine with fish and poultry – were agreed by most wine-drinkers after years of pleasurable experimentation. And you'll soon find out for yourself what wines you enjoy with different foods.

Because the pairing of food and wine is so much a matter of commonsense and personal taste, the following notes are intended only to be used as a guide.

• Traditionally the wine used in the preparation of a dish is the wine that should be served with it – even if it's Champagne.

• Pair regional dishes with regional wines: pasta in a meat sauce with Chianti; boeuf bourguignonne with a red burgundy; sauerkraut and sausages with an Austrian Gewürztraminer; carpetbag steak (with oysters) with an Australian Cabernet Sauvignon; goulash with a Hungarian Bull's Blood; paella (made with meat or fish) with a red or white Rioja; and so on.

• Some foods, though, will spoil your enjoyment of the wine in your glass, making it taste sour and harsh. Avoid serving a good wine with the following: salads dressed with a sharp vinaigrette (if this is a separate salad course in a meal, accompany the salad with bread; a salad main dish could be served with a dry rosé or light fruity red); most egg dishes (though a light wine – red or white – could go well with a cheese omelette or scrambled eggs and smoked salmon); spicy foods such as curry (a glass of beer or water is better, but if you want wine choose a strong white such as an Alsace Gewürztraminer or Sancerre); oily fish (full-bodied red wine is the mistake here; it really won't be a pleasant combination, but light, somewhat acidic reds could be served); strong cheeses (these will overwhelm a light wine, so serve with a hearty, full-bodied wine); rich desserts (medium-sweet or sweet whites are delicious with puddings, but red wines are not); desserts based on chocolate or lemon (these really won't bring out the best in any wine so it's better to serve them with coffee).

COOKING WITH WINE

The use of wine in cooking has a long history, and it is easy to see why. A judicious amount of wine added to a dish – sweet or savoury – can work wonders. And besides the flavour it imparts, wine also has a tenderizing effect on meat.

Any decent dry white or red wine is suitable for savoury cooking – decent meaning that it must be good enough to drink. Remember that cooking will drive off the alcohol in the wine, leaving just its flavour, and if that is sour and unpleasant it will spoil the dish.

In addition to dry table wines, fortified wines, dessert wines and grape-based spirits such as brandy are all excellent and versatile ingredients in the kitchen.

Here are some tips to using wine imaginatively in cooking:

• add a spoonful or two of medium sherry to a cheese sauce.

• a splash of red or white wine will jazz up a meat or poultry gravy; Marsala is excellent in gravy for chicken or turkey.

• marinate red meats and game in red wine, and poultry and white meats in white wine; this will flavour and tenderize the meat. Use the marinade in cooking the dish.

• stir a little dry or medium sherry or Madeira into soups such as consommé.

• use red vermouth, medium sherry or Marsala to make a simple pan sauce for veal escalopes.

• use a dessert wine such as Muscat de Beaumes de Venise or Sauternes in a fruit salad instead of a sugar syrup.

• rich, sweet port will enhance fools and mousses.

Wine Cups and Punches

TROPICAL COOLER

- 100 g (4 oz) caster sugar
- 12 ml (4 fl oz) lemon juice
- 1 bottle dry white wine
- ½ bottle golden or white rum
- 1 can crushed pineapple
- seasonal fruit, to garnish

Stir the caster sugar with the lemon juice until dissolved. Add the wine, rum and crushed pineapple and stir to mix. Cover and chill for several hours.

When ready to serve, add ice cubes and garnish with fruit.
SERVES 12

CARDINAL PUNCH

- juice of 6 lemons
- 225 g (8 oz) icing sugar
- 300 ml (½ pint) brandy
- 300 ml (½ pint) white rum
- 1 litre (1¾ pints) claret
- 150 ml (¼ pint) sweet vermouth
- 300 ml (½ pint) strong black tea
- 1 glass of sparkling wine (about 120 ml/4 fl oz)
- 450 ml (¾ pint) soda water
- seasonal fruits, to garnish

Stir together the lemon juice and sugar until the sugar has dissolved. Add the brandy, rum, claret, vermouth and tea and stir to mix. Pour over a large block of ice in a punch bowl and add the sparkling wine and soda water. Garnish with fruit and serve.
SERVES 18-20

SPARKLING SORBET PUNCH

- 500 ml (18 fl oz) lemon sorbet
- ½ bottle sweet or medium-sweet white wine, chilled
- 1 bottle sparkling white wine, chilled
- lemon slices, to garnish

Scoop the sorbet into a punch bowl. Add the wine and garnish with lemon slices. Serve immediately.
SERVES 8

From left: a cupful of Cardinal punch; a truly Tropical cooler; a delightful Summer fruit cup; a tingling Sparkling sorbet punch; a tantalizing Sangria

SUMMER FRUIT CUP

- 4 measures Grand Marnier

- 4 measures Kirsch or cherry brandy

- 350 g (12 oz) ripe summer fruits such as peaches, apricots, nectarines and strawberries, prepared and sliced

- orange and lime slices

- 1 bottle medium dry white wine, chilled

Combine the Grand Marnier, Kirsch or cherry brandy, summer fruits and orange and lime slices in a bowl. Stir, then cover and chill for about 1 hour. Add the wine and sti to mix.
SERVES 8

SANGRIA

- 4 tbls triple sec (see page 37)

- 100 g (4 oz) caster sugar

- 1 orange, thinly sliced

- 1 bottle chilled rosé wine

- 1½ bottles light or medium-bodied red wine, such as Rioja

- 300 ml (½ pint) orange juice

Combine the triple sec, 50 g (2 oz) of the sugar and the orange in a mixing bowl. Stir to dissolve the sugar, then cover and chill for 30 minutes.

Tip the orange mixture into a punch bowl or large jug and add the remaining ingredients. Stir well to mix and dissolve the sugar. Taste and add more sugar if you would like a sweeter punch. Add ice cubes and serve.
SERVES 18

SCANDINAVIAN GLÖGG

- 2 bottles dry red wine, or 1 bottle red wine and 1 bottle port or Madeira

- 50 g (2 oz) orange peel

- 20 cardamom pods, lightly crushed

- 2 cinnamon sticks

- 20 whole cloves

- 175 g (6 oz) blanched almonds

- 225 g (8 oz) raisins

- 225-350 g (8-12 oz) sugar cubes

- 300 ml (½ pint) brandy or Aquavit

Put the wine into a saucepan. Tie the orange peel and spices in a piece of muslin, add to pan. Add the almonds and raisins. Cook just below boiling point for 25 minutes, stirring occasionally.

Place a wire rack over the pan and spread out the sugar cubes on it. Warm the aquavit or brandy and pour it over the sugar cubes to saturate them all evenly. Set them alight: they will melt through the wire rack into the wine. Stir the glögg, then remove the spice bag. Serve hot, adding a few raisins and almonds to each cup.

SERVES 14

SHERRY COBBLER

- 1 tsp icing sugar

- 2 measures soda water or water

- 2 measures sherry

- fresh fruit slices, to garnish

Combine sugar and water in a wine glass. Stir to dissolve sugar. Add ice and sherry and garnish with fruit.

SERVES 1

QUICK SPICED RED WINE

- 600 ml (1 pint) dry red wine
- 600 ml (1 pint) water
- 100 g (4 oz) caster sugar
- 1 tsp whole cloves
- 1 cinnamon stick
- 4 cardamom pods, lightly crushed
- 1 mace blade (optional)
- 25 g (1 oz) sultanas

Combine the wine, water, sugar and spices in a saucepan and heat, stirring to dissolve the sugar. Bring to just below boiling point (do not boil) and cook for 10 minutes.

Strain the wine and discard the spices, then return the wine to the pan. Add the sultanas and cook for a further 3 minutes.
SERVES 4-6

BISHOP

- juice of ¼ lemon
- juice of ¼ orange
- 1 tsp icing sugar
- medium-bottled red wine such as claret (about 120 ml/4 fl oz)
- 3 dashes white rum or brandy (optional)
- orange and lemon slices, to garnish

Combine the lemon and orange juices and sugar in a highball glass or squat tumbler and stir to dissolve the sugar. Add 2-3 ice cubes and fill the glass with wine. Float rum or brandy on top and garnish with orange and lemon slices or twists.
SERVES 1

KIR

- 6 measures dry white wine
- ½ measure crème de cassis

Combine wine and crème de cassis in a large wineglass and stir. Add ice cubes, if liked.
SERVES 1

Kir punch: Macerate 225 g (8 oz) ripe but firm strawberries in 1-2 measures of crème de cassis for 1-2 hours. Add 3 bottles of chilled dry white wine and stir. If liked, fizz with some chilled soda water
SERVES 18-20

From left: a cool Sherry Cobler; Bishop; a refreshing Kir; Quick spiced red wine; Scandinavian Glögg

COCKTAILS

The practice of mixing different alcoholic drinks together to make a cocktail has a long history. Such drinks were certainly popular in 17th century Europe, and it is likely that the barman's art began long before.

Mixing cocktails at home is a lot of fun – and you don't need a fully-stocked drinks cupboard or lots of unusual equipment. With the cocktails, serve some 'nibbles', which could range from the simplest nuts and crisps to tiny hot vol-au-vents and individual quiches. Remember, though, that salty foods will make your guests thirsty!

If you wish to reduce the quantity of a cocktail, decrease all the ingredients proportionately or you will spoil the flavour.

Basic Equipment

A corkscrew and bottle opener are essentials. So, too, is an accurate measure – either a graduated measuring glass or an American-style double-ended bar measure. The latter has a 'jigger' (1½ oz) on one side and a 'pony' (1 oz) on the other.

To mix drinks, you will need two types of container. For drinks that are stirred, a mixing glass – which could be a large tumbler – with a long-handled spoon is used; these stirred drinks retain their clarity. Cocktails that have a cloudy appearance are mixed in a shaker and then usually strained. The ideal strainer is made of stainless steel, with a wire spiral surround to keep back the ice in the mixing glass or shaker. The third piece of equipment used to mix some drinks is an electric blender.

Glasses

No home barman could be expected to have a complete set of glasses for cocktails, but a basic selection should be on hand. For short drinks such as Martinis, requiring a stemmed glass, the classic cocktail shape – triangular with a wide, open top – is ideal; these glasses hold 3-4 oz. A tall tumbler or collins glass is needed for many long drinks such as Tom Collins and Highballs. A squat tumbler, holding 4-5 oz, like a whisky glass, is suitable for Old-fashioneds. In addition, wine glasses are suitable for many cocktails.

You should chill the glasses so that drinks will be kept cool as long as possible. Keep them in the refrigerator for 1 hour, or in the freezer for 5-10 minutes, before using. To frost a glass, store it in the freezer for 10-20 minutes.

Ice for cocktails

Ice is an essential component in a good cocktail, whether the ice is strained out after mixing or served in the glass. Recipes often call for cracked or crushed ice, and an electric or manual ice crusher makes this easy to achieve – or just wrap ice cubes in a towel and break them up with a hammer or mallet.

Garnishes

A garnish is added to a cocktail to give flavour and colour. Popular garnishes include maraschino cherries, stuffed green olives, cocktail onions and fresh fruit such as slices or wedges of orange, lemon or lime and spears of pineapple, as well as vegetables such as celery and cucumber. The classic garnish of a lemon twist is prepared as follows: thinly pare a piece of lemon peel about 2.5 × 1 cm (1 × 1½ inch) in size. Twist the lemon peel over the cocktail to release the oil, then drop the peel into the glass. You can rub the rim of the glass with the peel before you twist it.

There are also inedible garnishes added to cocktails – flowers, tiny paper parasols, herb sprigs, tiny paper flags, cocktail sticks and stirrers or swizzle sticks. Cocktails should be as much fun to look at as they are to mix and drink!

Amaretto di Saronno – an Italian dessert liqueur; almond flavoured.

Bitters – neutral spirits flavoured with bitter roots, aromatic herbs and spices and fruits, particularly orange and lemon; may be sweet, dry or actually bitter. Angostura is the most popular brand of bitters.

Campari – a bright red, pleasantly bitter apéritif, made in Italy.

Cream of coconut – thick cream available in tins.

Crème de banane – a dessert liqueur made with a cream base and banana flavour; and is bright yellow in colour.

Crème de cacao – a dessert liqueur with a chocolate flavour, made in France. Available white – actually colourless and clear – and dark brown. White is sweeter than brown.

Crème de cassis – a dessert liqueur with a blackcurrant flavour, made around Dijon, France.

Crème de menthe – a dessert liqueur with a mint flavour. Available white (colourless and clear) and bright green.

Cointreau – a dessert liqueur with an orange flavour, colourless and clear; made in France.

Curaçao – a dessert liqueur with an orange flavour. Available in a variety of colours: white (colourless and clear), orange-amber, blue, green, red and yellow.

Drambuie – a dessert liqueur based on Scotch whisky, flavoured with heather, honey and herbs.

Galliano – a sweet dessert liqueur, bright yellow in colour, and flavoured with herbs, berries, flowers and roots; made in Italy.

Grenadine – a sweet non-alcoholic syrup, flavoured with pomegranates and red in colour.

Kahlua – a dessert liqueur, flavoured with coffee, made in Mexico.

Madeira – see page 11

Maraschino – a dessert liqueur flavoured with cherry made primarily in Italy. Available clear or dark red.

Marsala – see page 11

Orgeat – a non-alcoholic syrup flavoured with almonds. Almond essence may be used instead.

Pernod – a clear, aniseed-flavoured apéritif made in France. When mixed with water, Pernod becomes 'milky'. Similar drinks are Ricard and anisette. All are called *pastis* in the South of France.

Port – see page 11

Sherry – see page 10

Southern Comfort – a dessert liqueur based on whiskey and flavoured with peaches; made in the United States.

Tia Maria – a dessert liqueur flavoured with coffee, with a hint of chocolate, made in Jamaica. Tia Maria is a little drier than Kahlua.

Triple sec – colourless and clear variety of curaçao (see entry left). Cointreau is the best known brand of triple sec.

LONG AND *Luscious*

These long, thirst-quenching drinks look deceptively innocent – but beware, some of them pack a hefty punch! Delicious and cooling, they are ideally suited to sip under a shady umbrella on a hot day. Try a Tequila Sunrise at sunset to usher in a mellow evening, a Planter's Punch for a taste of the tropics, or a Bloody Mary for its bite. But watch out for the harmless-looking Scorpion, with the gardenia floating serenely on its mild surface – after all, the scorpion does have a sting in its tail!

PIÑA COLADA

- 2 measures light rum
- 2 measures cream of coconut
- 3-4 measures pineapple juice
- 6-8 ice cubes, crushed
- fresh fruit, to garnish

Combine the rum, cream of coconut, pineapple juice and crushed ice in a blender. Blend at high speed for about 10 seconds. Pour into a chilled glass and garnish with slices of fresh fruit.
glass: tall tumbler, or collins glass

TEQUILA

This clear, strong spirit is distilled from the fermented mash or sap of the agave plant. It is made in Mexico, where it is usually consumed with a small ritual; it is drunk neat, chilled, followed by a taste of salt and then lime or lemon juice.

TEQUILA SUNRISE

- 2 measures tequila
- 4 measures orange juice
- ¾ measure grenadine

Combine the tequila and orange juice in a glass and stir. Add ice cubes. Slowly pour in the grenadine which will sink to the bottom, creating the 'sunrise'. Stir before drinking.
glass: tall tumbler or collins glass

From left: Tom Collins; Tequila Sunrise; Pina Colada

TOM COLLINS

The Tom Collins is an English original, created here in the late 19th century. The drink was first made with sweetened Old Tom gin – hence the name. The variation, John Collins, was originally made with Dutch gin, but is nowadays made with whisky.

- juice of ½ lemon
- 1 tsp icing sugar
- 2 measures gin
- soda water, chilled

TO GARNISH

- 1 lemon rind
- 1 maraschino cherry

Combine the lemon juice and sugar in a glass and stir until the sugar has dissolved. Stir in the gin. Add ice cubes and fill the glass with soda water. Garnish with the lemon and orange slices and the maraschino cherry.
glass: tall tumbler or collins glass

▶ V A R I A T I O N S :

John Collins:
use Scotch whisky or bourbon whiskey instead of gin.

Any basic spirit – rum, vodka, brandy – can be used instead of gin, in which case the drink is called a Rum Collins, etc.

BLOODY MARY

This popular Sunday brunch drink was probably created in the United States in the 1930s, and may have been named after Queen Mary I – although others say it was named for Mary Pickford, the famous Hollywood star of the thirties. The seasonings, like the name origins, may be altered to individual taste.

- 1½ measures vodka
- 3 measures tomato juice
- dash of lemon juice
- 1-2 dashes of Worcestershire sauce
- 2-3 drops of Tabasco sauce
- salt or celery salt and pepper
- celery stalk, to garnish

Combine vodka, tomato juice, lemon juice, Worcestershire sauce, Tabasco sauce, and salt or celery salt and pepper to taste and shake well. Strain into a glass. Add ice cubes if liked and garnish with the celery stalk.
glass: either a large wineglass or medium-sized tumbler

▶ VARIATIONS:

Bloody Maria:
use tequila instead of vodka.

Virgin Mary:
omit the vodka (a teetotal cocktail).

VODKA

Vodka was originally made from potatoes, but is now usually distilled from grain such as maize or barley. Russian protocol demands that the drinking of vodka (neat and chilled) must be preceded by a toast. The vodka is then dispatched in a single gulp.

HARVEY WALLBANGER

Apparently the name arises from the story of one Harvey who often consumed too many of these, and ended up banging into the walls!

- 1-2 measures vodka
- 4 measures orange juice
- ½ measure Galliano

Pour the vodka and orange juice into a glass. Add ice cubes and stir. Float Galliano on top.
glass: tall tumbler, or collins glass

PLANTER'S PUNCH

This cocktail originated in Jamaica.

- juice of 2 limes
- 2 tsp icing sugar
- 2 measures golden or white rum
- 1-2 measures soda water

TO GARNISH

- lime slice
- stick of fresh pineapple
- maraschino cherry

Combine the lime juice and sugar in a glass and stir until the sugar has dissolved. Stir in the rum. Add small ice cubes and fill the glass with soda water. Stir again. Garnish with fruit.
glass: tall tumbler or collins glass

SCORPION

- 1 measure white rum
- 1 measure brandy
- 2 measures orange juice
- 1 measure lemon juice
- ½ measure orgeat, or 2 tsp almond essence

TO GARNISH

- orange slice
- fresh mint sprig

Combine the rum, brandy, orange and lemon juices, orgeat or almond essence and some ice in a blender and blend at low speed for 15 seconds. Pour into a chilled glass over ice cubes and garnish with an orange slice and a sprig of mint.
glass: either a squat tumbler or old-fashioned glass

Titillate your taste buds, from left: Bloody Mary; Harvey Wallbanger; Planter's Punch; Scorpion

FLIPS AND *Fizzes*

Some of these drinks seem to have under-pinned the British Empire! The cooling fizzes are certainly ideally suited to the end of a blisteringly hot tropical day, with its abrupt and dramatic night-fall. What better drink than a Rickey when you are relaxing in your rattan chair on a cool and shaded verandah after a baking day on the rubber plantation? And a Singapore Sling is redolent of Raffles Hotel and the stories of Somerset Maugham – stories of witchcraft, adultery, debonair rogues and ruined reputations . . .

HIGHBALL

Although Scotch-and-soda has long been a popular drink, it wasn't until the 1890s that it gained the name Highball. Now Highballs are made with almost any spirit in combination with ginger ale or soda water or a host of other carbonated liquids.

- 2 measures Scotch or Canadian whisky or bourbon whiskey

- ginger ale or soda water

- lemon and lime slices, to garnish (optional)

Pour the whisky over ice cubes in a glass. Fill with ginger ale or soda water and stir gently. Garnish with lemon and lime slices, if liked.
glass: tall tumbler or highball glass

▶ VARIATION:

Presbyterian:
use bourbon whiskey and half ginger ale and half soda water.

BRANDY FLIP

The Flip, which originated in the United States, is a combination of spirit, whole egg and sugar shaken vigorously with ice and then strained. It can be made with many spirits instead of the brandy given here – port, sherry, and Marsala are also popular.

- 1½-2 measures brandy

- 1 egg

- 1 tsp icing sugar

- 2 tsp double cream (optional)

- chocolate curls

Shake the brandy, egg, sugar and cream vigorously with ice, then strain into a chilled glass. Sprinkle the top with a few chocolate curls.
glass: cocktail or other stemmed glass

AMERICANO

- 2 measures sweet vermouth
- 1 measure Campari
- soda water
- strip of lemon peel

Combine the vermouth and Campari in a glass. Add ice cubes and fill with soda water. Twist the lemon peel over the glass to decorate.
glass: large wine glass

MOSCOW MULE

- 1½ measures vodka
- juice of ½ lime
- ginger beer
- lime wedge, to garnish

Combine the vodka and lime juice in a glass. Add ice cubes and fill with ginger beer. Garnish with a lime wedge.
glass: tall tumbler such as collins glass, or beer mug (traditionally copper)

▶ VARIATION:

Use ginger ale instead of ginger beer.

A collection of classic cocktails, from left: Brandy Flip; Moscow Mule; Americano; Highball

SILVER FIZZ

- 2 measures gin
- juice of ½ lemon
- 1 tsp icing sugar
- 1 egg white
- soda water to top up
- orange and lemon, to garnish

Shake the gin, lemon juice, sugar and egg white with ice, then strain into a glass. Add ice cubes and soda water and stir. Garnish with orange and lemon.
glass: tumbler or collins glass, or large wine glass

▶ V A R I A T I O N :

Golden Fizz:
use a whole egg for this instead of just an egg white.

KISS-THE-BOYS-GOODBYE

- ¾ measure sloe gin (see page 47)
- ¾ measure brandy
- 1 tbls egg white
- juice of 1 lemon

Shake all the ingredients with ice and strain into a glass.
glass: cocktail or other stemmed glass

NEW ORLEANS FIZZ

- 2 measures gin
- 1½ measures double cream
- 1 tbls egg white
- 1 tbls lemon juice
- 1 tbls caster sugar
- 3 dashes of orange-flower water
- 2 measures soda water
- fresh fruit, to garnish

Combine the gin, cream, egg white, lemon juice, sugar and orange-flower water in a blender with some crushed ice. Blend for about 10 seconds. Add soda water and blend again, then strain into a glass. Garnish with fresh fruit.
glass: cocktail or other stemmed glass

A fistful of fizzes, from left: Kiss-the-boys-Goodbye; Silver Fizz; New Orleans Fizz; Singapore Sling

SINGAPORE SLING

- 1 tsp icing sugar or grenadine
- juice of ½ lemon
- 1½-2 measures gin
- soda water
- ½ measure cherry brandy
- fruits in season, to garnish

If using icing sugar, combine it with the lemon juice in a glass and stir until the sugar has dissolved. Stir in the gin, and grenadine if using. Add small ice cubes or crushed ice and fill the glass with soda water. Float cherry brandy on top and garnish with fresh fruits.
glass: tall tumbler or collins glass

GIN

Gin is distilled from fermented grains and usually receives its flavour and aroma from juniper berries. It was invented in Holland around 1600, but it was the English who made it so universally known; sweeter and very much cheaper than the gin of today, it became the opiate of the poor, hence the nickname 'mother's ruin'. London Dry Gin is now the most widely-consumed gin in the world. Other gins include Dutch gin (genever), which is drunk neat, Old Tom gin, Plymouth gin and sweet gins flavoured with orange, lemon or mint.

BUCK'S FIZZ

- 2 measures orange juice
- chilled champagne
- orange wedge, to garnish

Pour the orange juice into a glass over 2-3 ice cubes and fill with champagne. Stir gently to mix. Garnish with an orange wedge.
glass: large wine glass

▶ VARIATIONS:

Bellini:
use 2 measures of peach juice instead of orange juice and crushed ice instead of ice cubes. Garnish with a slice of fresh peach, if liked.

Caribbean Champagne:
use ½ tsp each light rum and crème de banane instead of orange juice, and serve in a champagne glass. Garnish with a slice of banana.

Luxury Cocktail:
combine 3 measures each brandy and champagne with 2 dashes of bitters in a container. Stir and pour into a champagne glass.

Mimosa:
use 4 measures each of orange juice and champagne.

A buoyant crop of cocktails slipping from left: Sloe Gin Rickey; Buck's Fizz; Cuba Libre. See above right on how to make your own Sloe gin

SLOE GIN RICKEY

A Rickey is a cross between a Collins and a Sour. Its basic ingredients are lime juice and soda water (or another carbonated drink), but the spirit may be gin, whisky, rum or brandy, or sloe gin.

- 2 measures sloe gin (see below)
- juice of ½ lime
- soda water
- lemon wedge, to garnish

Combine the sloe gin and lime juice in a glass. Add ice cubes. Fill with soda water and stir gently to mix. Garnish.
glass: tall tumbler or highball glass

SLOE GIN

To make sloe gin: gather 500 g (1 lb) autumn sloeberries. Pierce the skins and half fill bottles with berries and an equal weight of sugar. Top up with gin, seal and store for 2 months, shake occasionally. (See pages 44 and 59).

CUBA LIBRE

- ½ lime
- 2 measures white rum
- cola
- Lime wedge and fresh cherries, to garnish

Squeeze the juice from half a lime into a glass, then drop in a piece of lime. Add rum and ice cubes and fill with cola. Stir gently to mix. Garnish with a lime wedge and cherries, if using.
glass: tall tumbler or highball glass

COOL
AND
Deadly

These cocktails recreate the spirit of Prohibition America, when the Jazz Age was reaching its dizzy height. Millions of gallons of bootleg liquor were distilled all over the country, and bootleggers shot it out for the profits in the fast-proliferating speakeasies. While the gangsters and their molls are long dead and the Prohibitionists laid to waste, the Jazz Age no more than a faint echo, these drinks still carry the flavour of those days when daring and sophistication were all.

MANHATTAN

The Manhattan is thought to have been created around the turn of the century in New York City. Originally the sweet cocktail did not contain bitters.

- 2 measures Canadian whisky

- 1 measure sweet red vermouth

- dash of bitters

- fresh cherries, to garnish

Combine the whisky, vermouth and bitters in a container with ice and stir to mix. Strain into a glass and garnish with 2 cherries over the edge of the glass.
glass: cocktail or other stemmed glass

▶ VARIATIONS:

Bronx:
use gin instead of whisky, half sweet vermouth and half dry vermouth, and add the juice of ¼-½ orange.

Rob Roy:
use Scotch instead of Canadian whisky.

Dry Manhattan:
use dry vermouth instead of sweet.

RUM

Rum is distilled from the fermented juice of sugar cane or from molasses. It originated in the West Indies where, apart from being used in every conceivable way in cooking as well as drinking, it was also mixed with coconut oil and used to prevent nappy rash! There are three main types: light, golden and dark.

OLD-FASHIONED

- 1 small sugar lump
- dash of bitters
- 1 tsp water
- 2 measures Canadian whisky or bourbon whiskey

TO GARNISH

- strip of lemon peel
- maraschino cherry
- orange, lemon or lime slice

Combine sugar, bitters and water in a glass and 'muddle' (crush to mix). Add whisky and stir. Add ice cubes. Garnish with lemon, orange and cherry.
glass: either a squat tumbler or old-fashioned glass

In a celebratory mood for drinking? Try from left: Manhattan; Old fashioned; Pink Lady

PINK LADY

This is one of the great classic gin-based cocktails.

- 1½-2 measures gin
- 1 egg white
- 1 tsp grenadine
- 1 tsp double cream
- fresh strawberry, to garnish

Combine the ingredients in a container with ice and shake vigorously. Strain into a glass. Garnish with a halved strawberry on a cocktail stick.
glass: cocktail or other stemmed glass

▶ **VARIATION:**

White Lady:
use 2 measures of gin and ¾ measure each of Cointreau and lemon juice. Add 1 egg white if liked, and omit the grenadine and cream.

MARTINI

This famous cocktail, which made its debut in the United States as long ago as the 1860s, was first made with two parts gin to one part of vermouth. However, the Martini has become drier and drier, and some people now prefer it made with six parts gin to one part vermouth, or even with a ratio of ten to one. Do not shake the Martini with ice or it will turn cloudy.

- 1½ measures gin

- ¾ measure dry vermouth

- strip of lemon peel or stuffed green olive, to garnish

Pour the gin into a container of crushed ice. Add vermouth and stir briefly. Strain into a frosted glass and add twisted lemon peel or an olive.
glass: cocktail

▶ VARIATIONS:

Dry Martini:
use 1⅔ measures gin and ⅓ measure vermouth.

Extra Dry Martini:
use 2 measures gin and ¼ measure vermouth.

Sweet Martini:
use 1 measure gin and 1 measure sweet vermouth. Garnish with a twist of orange peel or a maraschino cherry.

Vodka Martini:
use vodka instead of gin.

Tequini:
use tequila instead of gin.

GIMLET

- 2 measures gin

- 1 measure unsweetened lime cordial

- 1 lime slice

Combine the gin and lime cordial in a container with ice and shake to mix. Strain into a glass and garnish with a lime slice.
glass: cocktail or other stemmed glass

▶ VARIATION:

Vodka Gimlet:
use vodka instead of gin.

A vibrant display from left: Martini; Rusty Nail; Gimlet; Brave Bull

BRAVE BULL

- 1½ measures tequila

- 1½ measures Kahlua or Tia Maria

- strip of lemon peel, to garnish

Combine the tequila and Kahlua or Tia Maria in a container with ice and stir to mix. Strain into a glass, add ice and garnish with twisted lemon peel.
glass: either a squat tumbler or old-fashioned glass

RUSTY NAIL

- 2 measures Drambuie

- 1 measure Scotch whisky

Pour the Drambuie and whisky into a glass over ice cubes and stir together gently to mix.
glass: either a squat tumbler or old-fashioned glass

▶ VARIATION:

Use equal measures of Drambuie and whisky.

51

WHISKY SOUR

The classic Sour cocktail was originally made with brandy when it was first introduced in the 1860s. The substitution of whisky for brandy was made some 30 years later, and the Whisky Sour quickly became a great hit – so much so that a glass of a special shape was named for the cocktail.

- 2 measures Canadian or Scotch whisky

- juice of ½ lemon

- ½-1 tsp icing sugar

TO GARNISH

- maraschino cherry

- orange or lemon slice

Combine the whisky, lemon juice and sugar in a container with ice and shake to mix. Strain into a glass and garnish with a cherry and an orange or lemon slice.
glass: sour glass or large wine glass

▶ V A R I A T I O N S :

Other spirits – rum, bourbon, gin, tequila or brandy – can be used instead of whisky, and the cocktail is then named after the spirit you have used (Rum Sour, etc.).

Watch your step! Sliding from the right: Stinger; Whisky Sour; Depth Bomb; Sidecar

BRANDY

Brandy is a strong spirit distilled from the fermented juice of grapes. The finest include Cognac and Armagnac from France. Spirits distilled in a different way are Grappa (Italy) and Calvados (France).

STINGER

- 1½ measures brandy

- ½ measure white crème de menthe

- mint sprig, to garnish

Combine the ingredients in a container with ice and shake to mix. Strain into a glass and garnish with mint.
glass: cocktail or other stemmed glass

SIDECAR

The Sidecar is thought to have made its first appearance in Paris during World War I, and was once very popular.

- 2 measures brandy
- 1 measure triple sec
- ½ measure lemon juice
- lemon and lime twists, to garnish

Combine the ingredients in a container with ice and shake to mix. Strain into a glass and garnish with lemon and lime.
glass: cocktail or other stemmed glass

DEPTH BOMB

This cocktail is also sometimes called a Depth Charge.

- 1½ measures brandy
- 1½ measures Calvados (a dry spirit based on apples)
- 2 dashes of lemon juice
- dash of grenadine
- fresh apple, to garnish

Combine the ingredients in a container with ice and shake to mix. Strain into a glass over ice cubes. Cut an apple into a 'chevron' shape and fix it on to the rim of the glass.
glass: squat tumbler or old-fashioned glass

SULTRY AND *Exotic*

This is the chapter for those who like Arabian nights, Caribbean carnivals and Polynesian sands. Sip a Zombie and imagine a tropical moon, the trade winds blowing softly through the palm trees and the sound of a steel band in the distance . . . Or try a Mai Tai and dream of flower garlands, palm trees and the blue of the Pacific. But perhaps your taste is for chiller climes; a Black Russian will conjure up a luxurious journey on the Orient Express – maybe with some sinister travelling companions . . .

CRUSTA

- small piece of lemon
- caster sugar
- ½ lemon
- 2 measures brandy
- ½ measure triple sec
- 1 tsp maraschino liqueur or grenadine
- 1 tsp lemon juice
- 1-2 dashes of bitters

Rub the rim of a glass with a piece of lemon to moisten it, then dip in sugar to coat the rim evenly. Discard the piece of lemon. Thinly pare the rind from ½ lemon in a spiral and place in the glass. Combine the brandy, triple sec, maraschino, lemon juice and bitters in a container with ice and shake to mix. Strain into the glass.

glass: cocktail or other stemmed glass

Open the treasure chest to discover from left: Adonis; Daiquiri; Crusta

ADONIS

- 2 measures dry sherry
- 1 measure sweet red vermouth
- 1-2 dashes of bitters
- orange and nectarine, to garnish

Combine the sherry, vermouth and bitters in a container with ice and stir to mix. Strain into a glass and garnish with a slice of orange and nectarine.
glass: either a cocktail or other stemmed glass

DAIQUIRI

The original version of this cocktail was invented around the turn of the century in Daiquiri, Cuba. The more modern frozen version is often made using fresh fruits such as banana, peach, strawberry, kiwi fruit or pineapple.

- 2 measures white rum
- ½-1 measure lime juice
- 1 tsp icing sugar
- lime slices, to garnish

Combine the ingredients in a container with ice and shake vigorously to mix. Strain into a glass and garnish with lime.
glass: cocktail or other stemmed glass

▶ VARIATIONS:

Frozen Daiquiri:
use 2 measures of lime juice and add 1 tsp of Cointreau or white curaçao. Combine the ingredients in a blender with 6 crushed ice cubes and blend at medium speed for 20 seconds. Serve in a champagne or wine glass.

Banana Daiquiri:
use 1½ measures of rum, 1½ measures of lime juice, 1 tbls of Cointreau or white curaçao, 1 ripe banana and 8-10 crushed ice cubes. Blend at medium speed for 15 seconds. Serve in a large wine glass.

Peach Daiquiri:
use 1½ measures of rum, ½ measure of lime juice, ½ canned or fresh peach, 1 tsp of icing sugar and 4-5 crushed ice cubes. Blend at medium speed for 10-15 seconds. Serve in a large wine glass.

BLACK RUSSIAN

- 2 measures vodka

- 1 measure Kahlua or Tia Maria

Pour the ingredients into a glass over ice cubes and stir gently to mix.
glass: either a squat tumbler or old-fashioned glass

▶ VARIATIONS:

Black Magic:
add a few drops of lemon juice and shake all the ingredients with ice. To serve, strain into a glass.

White Russian:
use white crème de cacao instead of Kahlua, and add 2 tsp double cream. Shake ingredients with ice and strain into cocktail or other stemmed glass.

A sophisticated quartet from left: Zombie; Black Russian; Margarita; Mai Tai

MARGARITA

- 1½ measures tequila

- ½ measure triple sec

- 1 measure lime or lemon juice

- salt

Rub the rim of a glass with lime or lemon peel, then dip into salt to coat the rim. Combine the tequila, triple sec and lime or lemon juice in a container with ice and shake to mix. Strain into the salt-rimmed glass.
glass: cocktail or other stemmed glass

ZOMBIE

The Zombie is very strong, as it contains the highest percentage of alcohol of all cocktails.

- 2 measures white rum
- ½ measure dark rum
- ½ measure apricot brandy
- 1 measure unsweetened pineapple juice
- 1 measure passion fruit juice
- juice of 1 lime
- juice of 1 small orange
- 1 tsp icing sugar
- 151-proof rum (optional)

TO GARNISH

- fresh pineapple wedge
- ½ orange slice
- maraschino cherry

Combine the light and dark rums, apricot brandy, fruit juices and sugar in a blender with 4-5 crushed ice cubes. Blend at low speed for 1 minute, then strain into a glass. Carefully float a little 151-proof rum on top, if using. Garnish with the pineapple, orange and cherry.
glass: tumbler or old-fashioned glass, or 300 ml (½ pint) zombie glass

MAI TAI

Trader Vic, who has a chain of Polynesian-style restaurants all over the world, claims to have invented this cocktail in the 1940s. The Mai Tai is sometimes served with an orchid floating on the top to add an exotic touch, but it is probably not wise to do this yourself.

- 2 measures dark rum
- ½ measure triple sec
- ½ measure apricot brandy
- juice of ½ lime
- 1 tsp grenadine

TO GARNISH

- fresh pineapple wedge
- maraschino cherry

Combine the rum, triple sec, brandy, lime juice and grenadine in a container with ice and shake to mix. Strain into a glass over crushed ice and garnish with pineapple and cherry.
glass: large tumbler or collins glass, or large old-fashioned glass

▶ VARIATION:

Increase the triple sec to 1 measure and omit the apricot brandy; increase the grenadine to 1 tbls; and add 1 tbls orgeat or almond essence.

WHISKY

There are several different varieties of whisky apart from Scotch available. Irish whiskey is usually blended and is more full-bodied than Scotch. Canadian whisky is also blended, and is very smooth and light in flavour. Bourbon whiskey, from Kentucky, is made from a fermented mash of grains that by law must be not less than 51 per cent maize. Rye whiskey contains at least 51 per cent rye. In Ireland and the USA whiskey is spelt with an 'e'. (More overleaf.)

SLOW *Sippers*

These colourful drinks are for savouring slowly, whether you prefer a cold-climate classic such as Bullshot or Brandy Alexander or a more exotic tipple such as Blue Hawaiian or even an ostentatious Golden Cadillac. The Grasshopper, as its name suggests, is simply a drink of cheerful frivolity, a Sicilian Kiss is sweet and heady while the Mint Julep has overtones of the Southern Belles in the great plantation houses of the American Deep South. Whatever your choice, be sure to take it good and slow . . .

MINT JULEP

The Mint Julep is a traditional drink in the southern states of the US, where it was originally a non-alcoholic minted fruit drink.

- 1 tsp icing sugar

- few drops of cold water

- 6-8 fresh mint sprigs

- 2½-3 measures bourbon whiskey

Combine the sugar, water and 4-5 mint sprigs in a glass and crush gently to release the flavour from the mint and dissolve the sugar. Fill the glass with shaved or crushed ice and add the bourbon. Stir gently to mix, then garnish with the remaining mint sprigs.
glass: tall tumbler or collins glass or silver mug with handle

▶ VARIATIONS:

Crush the sugar, water and mint sprigs in a container, then pour into a frosted glass. Use brandy instead of bourbon.

SLOE 'N' COMFORTABLE

- ¾ measure sloe gin
- ¾ measure Southern Comfort
- 3 measures orange juice
- maraschino cherry, to garnish

Combine the sloe gin, Southern Comfort and orange juice in a glass. Add ice and stir to mix. Garnish with a cherry.
glass: tall tumbler or highball glass

▶ VARIATION:

Sloe Screw: use 1½ measures of sloe gin and omit the Southern Comfort.

BULLSHOT

This is supposed to be a good hangover cure! As a variation, you can serve it hot – presumably best if you have a hangover on a cold morning!

- 1½ measures vodka
- 4 measures beef consommé
- dash of Worcestershire sauce
- salt and pepper

Combine the ingredients in a container with ice and shake to mix. Strain into a glass (handled, if hot).
glass: large wineglass or handled glass

WHISKY

Whiskies are distilled from a fermented mash of grain, usually barley, wheat, rye or maize, and aged in barrels. Scotch malt whisky, the *doyenne* of whiskies, is made using the traditional pot still method, from malted barley dried over peat fires. Up until a hundred years ago, brandy was the preferred spirit, but the devastation of the European vineyards by the disease phylloxera made it scarce and whisky came into its own. More whisky facts on page 57.

Take it nice 'n' easy from left: Bullshot;
Sloe 'n' Comfortable; Mint Julep

Sheer delight, from left: Sicilian Kiss; Blue Hawaiian; Golden Cadillac; Brandy Alexander; Grasshopper

SICILIAN KISS

- 2 measures Southern Comfort

- 1 measure Amaretto di Saronno

- slice of lemon, to garnish

Combine in a glass with plenty of crushed ice and stir to mix. Garnish with a slice of lemon.
glass: either a squat glass or old-fashioned glass

BLUE HAWAIIAN

- 2 measures white rum

- ½ measure blue curaçao

- ½ measure triple sec

- ¾ measure double cream

- 1 tsp cream of coconut

Combine the ingredients in a container with ice and shake thoroughly to mix. Strain into a glass.
glass: cocktail or other stemmed glass

BRANDY ALEXANDER

- 1 measure brandy
- 1 measure white crème de cacao
- 1 measure double cream
- grated nutmeg

Combine the brandy, crème de cacao and cream in a container with ice and shake vigorously for a few moments. Strain into a glass and sprinkle the top with a pinch of nutmeg.
glass: either a cocktail or other wide stemmed glass

▶ VARIATION:

Alexander's Sister:
use gin instead of brandy and crème de menthe instead of crème de cacao.

GOLDEN CADILLAC

- 1 measure Galliano
- 1-2 measures white crème de cacao
- 1 measure double cream

Combine the Galliano, crème de cacao and double cream in a blender and blend at low speed for 10 seconds. Pour into a glass.
glass: either a cocktail or champagne saucer glass

GRASSHOPPER

- 1 measure white crème de menthe
- 1 measure green crème de menthe
- 1 measure double cream

Combine the ingredients in a container with ice and shake for a few seconds. Strain into a glass.
glass: cocktail or other stemmed glass

▶ VARIATION:

Flying Grasshopper:
use ¾ measure each of green and white crème de menthe and 1 measure of vodka, and omit the cream.

61

WARM AND *Glowing*

These are the drinks to warm you through and through on a cold winter's night. What better way to relax after skiing, skating or simply walking in the snow than by warming your toes at an open fire and sipping an Egg Nog? And there's no need to wait until you have a cold before treating yourself to a Hot Toddy in bed. A Brandy Blazer, the flames licking on its surface, is probably the most dramatic cocktail there is – an impressive finish to an intimate dinner – while Irish Coffee is one of the great classic drinks.

EGGNOG

- 1 egg
- 1 tsp caster sugar
- 1 measure brandy
- 1 measure golden or white rum
- 6-8 measures hot milk
- grated nutmeg

Combine the egg and sugar in a mug and stir to dissolve the sugar. Add the brandy, rum and hot milk, stirring constantly. Sprinkle with a pinch of nutmeg.

▶ VARIATIONS:

Cold Eggnog:
use 2 measures of brandy or whisky and omit the rum. Use 4 measures of chilled milk. Shake all the ingredients with ice and strain into a large wine glass or tumbler. Sprinkle with nutmeg.

Baltimore Eggnog:
use ¾ measure each of brandy, rum and Madeira. Prepare as above.

BRANDY BLAZER

- 1 sugar cube
- strip of orange peel
- strip of lemon peel
- 2-3 measures brandy

Combine the sugar with orange and lemon peels in a glass and crush to mix. Add the brandy and stir. Set alight and serve flaming.
glass: either a squat tumbler or old-fashioned glass

A hearty hoard of winter warmers, from left: Brandy Blazer; Irish Coffee; Hot Toddy; Eggnog

HOT TODDY

- 1 sugar cube
- 4-6 measures boiling water
- 2 measures whisky

TO GARNISH
- 1 lemon slice
- cinnamon stick

Place the sugar cube and boiling water in a mug and stir to dissolve the sugar Add the whisky and stir to mix. Garnish with a lemon slice and a stick of cinnamon for stirring.

▶ VARIATIONS:

Add ½ stick of cinnamon and 3 cloves. Use brandy, port, rum or gin instead of whisky. Use nutmeg not cinnamon.

IRISH COFFEE

Many other liqueurs and spirits can be substituted for Irish whiskey in this popular after-dinner drink. Cointreau or Grand Marnier, brandy and Tia Maria are excellent.

- 1-2 tsp caster sugar
- 5 measures strong black coffee
- 1½ measures Irish whiskey
- whipped or double cream

Combine the sugar and coffee in a glass and stir to dissolve the sugar. Add the whiskey, and top with whipped or double cream. If using double cream, pour it slowly onto the coffee over the back of a spoon so that it will float on the surface.
glass: large wine glass or other stemmed goblet

INDEX